THE UNNATURAL WEST

AN OVERVIEW

SIMON LENNON

The Unnatural West: An Overview
Non-Fiction (Ethics and Moral Philosophy, Humanism)
A book in the collection: The West
Published by Pine Hill Books

ISBN 978-1-925446-36-4 (electronic)
ISBN 978-1-925446-37-1 (paperback)
57,000 words
Cover image: London, 2004

In memory of my cousins
George and Elizabeth Clarke,
of Cirencester, Gloucestershire

CONTENTS

PREFACE

No race through history has felt about people as white men, women, and thus children now feel. No other race on earth feels so now. We neglect and mistreat each other while aiding everyone else, ultimately harming ourselves.

Examining how we came to this extraordinary situation and its implications is my collection of eleven non-fiction books titled *The West*, comprising four series of two or three books each: *Individualism*, *Identity*, *Nationalism*, and *Cultures*. This overview, *The Unnatural West*, collates into a single volume the principal ideas from the first series, *Individualism*, comprising:

1. *Western Individualism*.
2. *The End of Natural Selection*.
3. *The Need for Nations*.

This overview omits the foundations, evidence, and examples supporting those ideas, for which readers so interested may turn to those eleven books and their bibliographies. Generally, those foundations, evidence, and examples are in the book described by the chapter in which those ideas appear. For ease of reading and understanding, some ideas appear in other chapters of this overview and its companion overviews.

Much as the Far East means East Asian races, their cultures, and civilisations and the Middle East means Arabs, Jews, and their cultures and civilisations, so does the West mean peoples racially European, our cultures and civilisation. Whether Europeans are one race or several races and the West is one civilisation or several civilisations, such as English, Scottish, Welsh, and so forth, is a matter of nomenclature, as it is for other races and ethnicities. We could be said to be different European races but the same Western Civilisation.

Westerners are white people. People hostile to the West are hostile to white people, and vice versa. People defending one defend the other.

Please consider the ideas in this overview and the books. If the

West is going to progress from this Age of Ideology to a New Age of Enlightenment, an Age of Re-Enlightenment, back to reason, morality, and the pursuit of truth, we are going to have to learn again to consider ideas new to us. We will need again to discuss matters rationally with each other.

1. WESTERN INDIVIDUALISM

People are biological beings with natural instincts. Among those instincts, we are innately tribal: some people are our people and some people are not. It is more than a desire to be part of a herd less than every human or living being on earth. It is a sense that, in some definitive way, we already are.

Our natural herd is, at the very least, eight: the smallest group of which we are inherently part. Eight would represent a large nuclear family or a slightly extended family, although most tribes are much bigger than that. Tribes can be, for example, clans, nations, and races. We are not naturally individuals.

The West's problem is having lost faith in human nature and society, at least in ours. Primitive instincts and social forces have not changed. What changed is our attitude towards them.

We keep denying human nature or trying to change it. Where we cannot change human nature, we suppress it. We have the arrogance and stupidity to think we should rise above it.

Individuality

European races were already not like other races. All races value conformity, but we had a long history cherishing individuality. All races understood collective familial and tribal rights, without using such phrases, but we enjoyed individual rights too.

Individuality connoted each person's particular thoughts and feelings, likes and dislikes. They distinguished a person from the people around, not that we needed distinction. Each person's different beliefs and opinions underpinned democracy, liberalism, freedom of speech, and other Western inventions.

That liberalism is better known as classic liberalism, devoted to truth and reason, built upon the human condition trying to improve the human experience. For all its vaunting of individuality, classic liberalism remained for the most part Christian, nationalist, and racist, in the postmodern parlance. Fact and reason required it.

Individuality is not individualism. Colonial Europeans considered individualism to be a brave individual self-reliance against alien and physically hostile frontiers far from Europe. We rarely needed anyone's help, but stood together as nations and races when we did. The West in our glory days married Western individuality and frontier individualism with the co-operation of nationalism. Classic individualism was a nationalist individualism.

It was all very natural, because races differ and humans are tribal. The Great War shattered everything.

Losing Our Self-Belief

For a people who talk so much of the world, the West is stunningly ignorant of the forces affecting us. Of all the killing throughout the world since Cain killed Abel, the most influential upon our time, still driving Western values, were the two world wars.

We cannot understand the West since the Second World War without understanding that war in all its facets, but we cannot understand that war without understanding the First World War and its aftermath. If the seeds of Western decline were not the Great War, then they were the hubris that brought great nations into conflict and kept us there.

The familial links between monarchs should have avoided wars in Europe, but in 1914 we stared each other down. We blamed the Great War upon Germany, but she was no more responsible than other combatants. Pre-war alliances defensive in nature or informal need not have dragged any of us to war.

The assassination of Austrian Archduke Franz Ferdinand in Serbia in June 1914 was an internal Austro-Hungarian affair. So was the Austro-Hungarian Empire's response. Germany had no need to take an interest in that response.

The Russian Empire could have refused to intervene in the internal affairs of another empire. For being Austria-Hungary's internal affair, France and her empire could have refused to join Russia in that intervention.

Belgium could have granted Germany's request for passage through Belgium to France in August 1914. Britain could have declined Belgium's attempt to invoke the 1839 Treaty of London inviting Britain and our empire to war because Germany's incursion through Belgium was only as a thoroughfare for her invasion of France. Belgian forces need not have engaged German forces along their way.

Civilisation that previously seemed inviolable died in France in the Great War. It died in Belgium in 1914 when Germans, hitherto the most honourable of races, thought they could end the war quickly by frightening local villagers. They failed. If civilisation did not die in the Great War, it certainly began to fray.

Estimates vary, but fifteen or more million people died and more than twenty million were wounded through that incomprehensible four-year war and the malnutrition and disease it wreaked, with more casualties in the Russian Civil War it bequeathed. The Great War wasted the wealth Europeans engaged in the war had amassed since the Industrial Revolution.

Worse than that, amidst all the killing and dying, the West began losing faith in the natural order: in facts and human nature. In the killing fields of France, we lost our self-belief.

There were no victors from the Great War. With peace came less celebration than relief.

Cultures are intrinsic to civilisation. When we lost confidence in our civilisation, we lost confidence in our cultures. If they had not brought us into war, they had not saved us from it either. We ceased valuing our heritage and history, feeling we could not collectively do anything worthwhile.

In the 1919 Treaty of Versailles, France and her fellow victors punished a defeated Germany as if the Great War had been Germany's fault alone. In time, Germany rose from her rut and rot. She rebuilt her self-belief and became again impressive, until France, Britain, and their empires declared more war upon her in 1939. The peace previously supposed to be eternal was not.

The Great War became known as World War I, the First horrible World War, when World War II made world war repetitious. Tens of millions more Europeans and others died, including men, women, and children who had not enlisted to fight and die. Grand cities across Europe along with pretty towns and villages, testament to what had been a great civilisation, lay ruined.

The Second horrible World War scared us from ourselves: from ever wanting self-belief again. Europe's colonies and war-weary Europe herself came not to feel European, for fear we would think too well of ourselves. We came to dread where truth and nature, race and nation took us.

Everything about us fell from repute. Two world wars and a holocaust condemned us to a coincidence of disillusion, from which we have still not recovered.

Ideologies

Western Civilisation through its many manifestations was glorious, improving and improving, for the most part. We developed sciences, technologies, and innovations the like of which no other races have, along with arts, cultures, and philosophies extraordinary on earth.

Even the devastating French Revolution of 1789 sought to replace the old European order with a new Western Civilisation, much as the American Revolution from 1765 had talked of doing. Western humanism rejected super nature but not nature, turning from Christian countries towards ancient Greece and Rome, if without the super nature of ancient Greece and Rome. It was a pan-European school of thought: Europeanism, not really humanism, in place of Christianity and, to a degree, nationalism.

Rejecting the French Revolution for being bourgeois, nineteenth-century Jewish atheist Karl Marx rejected Western Civilisation altogether. Jewish humanism refuses Europeanism and nationalism, becoming the antithesis not just of theism, whether Jewish or Christian, but of natural tribalism.

Jewish humanism prevailed. Humanism became ideological.

Ideologues feel no racial or other tribal connection with the people upon whom they impose their ideologies. Perceiving people in ideological imagery, humanism dehumanises.

An idea becomes an ideology when people believe it or impose it without regard for the facts and without respect for human nature or other consideration of the impact upon people. If ideologies do not simply disregard human nature, they try to remake human nature in favour of an idealised vision of what human nature should be.

Ideologies are unnatural. Thus nativism, nationalism, Europeanism, and other tribalism are not ideologies.

People create and disseminate ideologies. Powerful people

impose them. Ideologies are thus political constructions. When enough people believe them, political constructions become social constructions.

Marxist communism was the original ideology. Marx and his atheist Prussian collaborator and benefactor Friedrich Engels published their *Manifesto of the Communist Party* in 1848.

Communism rejected racial, religious, and other natural delineations between people for distracting the poor from class conflict with the rich. A view of the world premised upon social and economic divisions opposed anything that united people across those divisions, as racial loyalty and collective religion did.

Collectivist cultures are racially and religiously homogenous because the only natural and thus meaningful collective identities are biological and theological. Race and religion matter because family and deity matter.

Marxism advocated collectivism across races and nations, without racial or religious loyalties, affinities, or identities: a multiracial irreligious collectivism. Mere sharing became ideological, among people without reason to share.

The Age of Ideology

While small numbers of people disillusioned with the West or hostile towards it may well have continued writing and talking about communism, Marxism might have never been put into place without the disastrous Great War. Promising a new world civilisation to those who had lost faith in Western Civilisation, as so many Europeans had through the Great War, communism found its footing in the fallen Russian Empire.

Having lost confidence in our countries and cultures, or in people and civilisation altogether, we sought confidence in ideology. All the assurances we once found from our race and ancestral religion, we began to find in political and economic opinion. Having lost faith in fact and reason, we came to find it in dreams and ideals. The Age of Ideology began.

From the fallen Russian Empire came the communist Soviet Union in 1922. Through World War II, the Soviet Union occupied Eastern Europe, imposing communism from 1945.

Elsewhere around the West, World War II empowered

ideologues previously kept in check. Losing our last faith in Western Civilisation, we let loud people persuade us to a second ideology: the ideology of individualism. Ideologies became our new Western sectarianism.

The important ideologies of the twentieth century were never Marxism or individualism. They were never communism or capitalism, to the extent that anyone adopted capitalism as an ideology. They were those overarching ideologies that deny the West the biological links between people and thus our natural commonalities: our tribes, nations, races, and collective religion.

Idealists might have imagined us overcoming our racial and religious affinities: our ancient tribal loyalties. Ideologues and our enemies set about erasing them.

Among the communist countries, collective interests across races failed. Without nationalism or other natural tribalism, collective interests within races also failed.

Some people are extraordinarily kind without a collective identity to inspire them. Most grow weary of people not so generous taking advantage of them. Without nationalism or other natural tribalism, communism eventually devolves to individualism.

There can be no global collectivism, although that has not stopped communists in their hostility to the West continuing to advocate it. Also advocating it are other races in their greed, wanting to take more Western wealth without reciprocating. The few communist countries outside the West retain their racial boundaries.

If communism remains or is again more attractive than individualism to people ignorant of communism everywhere it has been implemented, then it is because communism promises political and economic tribalism. It is simply unable in power to deliver upon its promises. The only meaningful tribalism is natural.

The globalism that best survived the twentieth century was individualism. Ours is the free market individualism equivalent to the secular humanism that failed under Soviet communism. Our relative success over communist collectivism in economic terms masks our equivalent failure in human terms: in moral, social, and other cultural terms.

Money is no substitute for civilisation. Neither is technology.

Without natural tribal identities, communities and families wither. Cultures abate. Morality, loyalty, and honour become obsolete.

Our interests are sordid self-interests. We alone comprise those selves.

The Age of Ideology has been among the most destructive eras in Western history: taking the good and making us bad, the kind and leaving us cruel. We keep moving on, putting poor experiences behind us, extraordinarily accepting of our lots in lives and the people around us: *their* selfishness and horribleness.

We became increasingly disconnected from our forebears and descendants, from each other and ourselves. We became the unnatural West.

Losing Our Tribes

We presume our rejection of racism and other biological tribalism is the result of research or discoveries amidst our endless enlightenment: a drawing back of past curtains from Western minds. It is not. It is a specific Western response to historical events. We are simply another passage of history.

Without the Great War, there would have been no Soviet communism. There would have been no Nazism, World War II, or Holocaust. There would be no ideological individualism. There would be no multiculturalism.

Ours is the era post Holocaust: the Jewish Holocaust during World War II. From 1941 until the end of the war in 1945, without anywhere else to send them, Nazi Germany and her allies in the endeavour killed in the order of six million Jews.

Even in spite of vivid memories of the mass slaughters of World War I and the rise of Nazism in Germany, without the mass killing of World War II, might there have not been a Jewish Holocaust? Might peace across Europe instead of war in 1941 have allowed the final solution to Germany's conflict with the Jews to be six million Jewish deportations to a Jewish homeland, such as Israel, instead of six million Jewish deaths?

Genocides normally shape their victims, but no other genocide affects the perpetrators as the Holocaust cuts a swathe through European races. It denies us the chance to be what other races remain.

The deep trauma of the Holocaust was not its brutality, but its civility. These were no barbarous Turks massacring two million Armenians where they found them, as Turks had done during and after the Great War. It was the most civilised of peoples, the Germans, from the most civilised races on earth, Europe's, methodically organising victims onto trains to their deaths. It was society and civilisation, and we lost our last faith in each of them.

We lost the distinction between good and bad societies, but *Obersturmbannführer* Bruno Müller recognised the distinction. He led a unit that killed a hundred and fifty-five Jews in the city of Bender, Moldova in 1941, but only trusted the men who had burnt "the bridges to respectable society" by murdering someone. When the West took up culpability for the Holocaust, we all burnt those bridges.

The Ideology of Individualism

Unfolding since World War II has been the new and uniquely Western ideology of individualism. If Marxism is a rejection of Western society and civilisation, then individualism is a rejection of any society and civilisation.

Not merely the differences between us and the people around us, individualism is our assertion, above all else, that we are not the people around us. We have become individuals: each person distinct from everyone else. Other people we denote individuals too. A person's identity is only that person, without reference to anyone else. I am just I. You are just you. He is just he. She is just she.

We are more likely to label it liberalism or neoliberalism, but liberalism before World War II was not like this. Classic Western liberalism became Western individualism when we, like the communists, lost our natural collective senses: nation, race, and collective religion.

Surrendering every sense of collective familial, racial, and other innate tribal interests leaves only naked individual interests, nothing else. The only selves the West now understands are individual selves. Without natural collective identities, we are mere individuals, without consideration or comprehension of being more than we already are, without thinking about it.

The loss of our nationalism, racism, and collective Christianity is our individualism. Being a global ideology, Western individualism gave rise to Western multiculturalism, Western capitalism, and our other calls for diversity: our postmodern globalism.

Individualism became the unnatural West's post-racial, post-Christian, post-national ideology. We try to make people what we think people should be, as there has never before been attempted among democracies, rather than cater to natural instincts we fear, not the least of all in ourselves.

Western individualism has become so pervasive, if only among us, we do not realise it is merely an idea: a shared ideology. Individualism could be our vision for what all people on earth should become, or our presumption of what they already are.

The unnatural West considers any delineation of the human species into peoples (such as racism, nationalism, and collective religion) to be divisive, but individualism is no less divisive. Without peoples, we treat everyone as individuals, but cannot possibly know everyone. So we dwell upon our own lives without the distractions that other people can be. If identifying with a group creates a sense of them and us, then not identifying with a group leaves just them and me, however fortunate we are to grab moments of just you and me.

The more we abandoned natural tribalism, the more insular we became. We went from nationalism to narcissism.

Too individually minded for bravery or heroism, our new ideology of individualism is more than merely not fighting a war alongside our compatriots. It is us not having to help them, nor them having to help us.

We might help our families or friends, if doing so does not impinge upon us, but have become less likely to help people whose paths we cross. Without societies to interfere, we have the right to neglect others as much as they have the right to neglect us.

There are those who defend individualism claiming it keeps us from war, but countries outside the West maintain their senses of society without war. Our lack of nationalism, racism, and other tribalism does not keep us from joining other people's wars or embarking upon new wars in other people's countries. It adds to them.

Neither does individualism save us from crime and terror. It exacerbates our vulnerability. The societies we are glad to have lost are societies of people saving each other.

Individualism is our isolation. We might no longer be so natural as to feel lonely, but we are alone.

Without races, nations, and collective Christianity, we have come inextricably to be discontent, mindlessly compliant with the edicts of others, deceitful, and estranged from the world beyond our individual selves. We are self-serving, self-absorbed, and ultimately self-destructive, preoccupied with what we consume and with each other's beliefs.

Conviction in us alone became a virtue, but even the most powerful of people become fragile when left alone. The rise of individualism has increasingly left us unhappy, lonely, and unable to cope with the changes around us.

We once were nations standing together in war, most notably Britain through the direst days and nights of the Battle of Britain. We have become individuals psychologically fragile.

Human Authorities

Our naïve noble nations' confidence in our leaders proved to be misplaced when those leaders blundered into the Great War and kept us there. The human authorities in whom the masses trusted failed us badly.

They failed us again in 1939. They are failing us again.

The authority of churches diminished with each world war. It diminished thereafter. God's role guiding the West diminished with it. Human authorities filled their spaces.

Humanism is premised upon trust in human authorities, but only particular human authorities. Those authorities are people without biological tribalism or religious belief, or at least any that they share with the people over whom they preside.

Our dictators are not common to us. They are tiny and elite.

Humanism proved particularly hostile to Christianity for curtailing the role of human authorities in people's lives. Roman Catholicism undermined human authority by according primary authority to the Church. Traditional Protestantism undermined human authorities and churches alike, by according primary authority to Scripture.

Communist authorities were state authorities, to which Marxism entrusted the people. Intellectuals, industrial workers, and peasants comprised classless collectives, which bureaucratic experts instructed to think and labour for everyone's betterment. People consumed only what they needed, as bureaucratic experts determined.

Marxism offered us all the choices we wanted, subject to human authorities deciding what we needed. Once those human authorities decided, the choices were not really ours to make.

The human authorities to which the free West meekly complied following World War II were more than just government. Most notably, they also included large corporations, universities, schools, courts, and other bodies, along with news media, film-makers, and television networks. Much as happened under communism, once those human authorities decided something, choices were not really ours to make.

Western churches succumbing to individualism and other ideology in place of Scripture became like other humanist authorities. Western Christianity became less of a problem.

Those free Western authorities might not have been at the behest of governments as they were in communist countries, but they might as well have been. The people dominating those authorities were much the same people as those dominating governments. We might label ours the upper class, aristocracy, establishment, or elite: political, business, and other leaders.

Before the two world wars, our Western elite saw themselves as the world's elite for being the elite of our races, countries, and the West. Without racism and nationalism, they increasingly became simply the world's self-supposed elite, feeling more in common with rich, famous, and powerful people of other races than with ordinary people of their own. The West declines while others rise, but they imagine themselves rising with others.

Their feeling is not reciprocated. The elite of other races continue identifying with their races, nations, and religions.

Exercising Authority

Traditional tribal authorities had tribal objectives, acting for the good of the tribe. They respected human biology, instinct, and relationship even while knowing very little about them. They deferred to whatever they believed God or the gods to want.

Outside the West, the legitimacy of any authority, whether democratic or not, even communist, still depends upon nationalism or other tribalism. Especially but not only in Islamic countries, authority often also depends upon religious devotion shared with the people. Governments, corporations, and other bodies must act, or at least claim to act, in the interests of the faith and country instead of themselves.

Nationalism and other tribalism connect leaders with the led, as compatriots and tribespeople reciprocate. The queens and kings to serve are those ruling with their people: nationalistic servants of the led.

Humanism is very different. At best, humanist authorities feel estranged from everyone. They represent not their nations but themselves and thus their individual and sectional interests. Without nationalism or other tribalism and without their religious heritage, human authorities pursue their particular personal political and economic objectives.

At worst, their racial, religious, or other tribal connection is with another race or religion altogether. Instead of neglecting us, they defend and advance that other race or religion. They might even deliberately work against us: making their decisions and imposing their ideologies intending to harm the people upon whom they impose those ideologies.

Soviet authorities were always humanist: communist. Free Western authorities became humanist: individualist.

Soviet state and other government instrumentalities could not manufacture a multiracial good or identity: a multiracial collectivism. At least they tried.

Western authorities never tried. Our leaders' indifference to our peoples that sustained war in Europe past 1914 and brought war to Europe in 1939 became individualism. It brought us multiculturalism.

Our problems were never racial and religious loyalties. Our problems were the lack of racial and religious loyalties, at least to us, among the people in charge.

In spite of the humanist claims otherwise, the West no longer believes in people, not our people. We might talk of faith in people, but our faith is in other people: other races.

Western authorities have had decreasing regard for Western nations, races, and our religious heritage since 1914 and especially since 1945, becoming increasingly contemptuous of them. Their regard is for themselves and for other races altogether.

Rejecting the will of our race, we now call leadership. Implementing the will of their race, other races call leadership.

Our churches and governments, not God or our countries, betrayed us. They deserved to lose their diminishing authorities.

Without biology or God in mind, the only semblance of authority remains with those few leaders in whom others have confidence in their abilities and with whom they share collective interests: something towards collective identities. They might, for example, be police and military units if not police and military forces overall, the most successful sporting teams, or casts and crews making films and performing plays.

Propaganda

It is hard for us to know what life was like before we came of age, behind the histories that schools, media, and entertainment convince us happened. People are confined by what they know, or what they are told.

Instead of bringing before people the facts so we can examine those facts as best as we can, deal with them as best as we can, Western authorities no longer bring before people the facts, not about anything important. We do not recognise the indoctrination of the West that began with communism in Soviet Russia and the Soviet Union after the Great War and worsened across the apparently free West after World War II.

For all our talk about freedom, human authorities manipulate people, inadvertently or otherwise, for political and commercial objectives. Soviet propaganda tried to drive people into being communists: connecting people who were not naturally connected. Western propaganda drives us deeper into individualism: separating people who are naturally connected.

In both environments, in the circumstances of both ideologies, propaganda wilfully or inadvertently separated and separates us from our families and race. It separates us from our religions and other cultures. It drives us apart and keeps us apart from human nature. It denies us our natural instincts.

Without a desire for the truth, people believe propaganda

because it suits them to believe it. People wanting reasons not to take interests in other people believe whatever excuses them from needing to take interests in other people: from moral responsibilities to help each other. That might be communism claiming that everything is good under communism. That might be individualism claiming that everything would be better without races and nations: without racism and nationalism. That might be commercial marketing.

The communist dictatorship's media control never achieved the uniformity of propaganda across the Soviet Union that free media achieved across America. As much from people and corporations as from governments, there has rarely if ever been more pervasive propaganda as that increasingly shaping the supposedly free West.

With well-written scripts to guide us, we believe whatever programmers and film-makers determine we believe. We become tolerant of whatever newscasters, programmers, and film-makers determine we tolerate. Storytellers espouse the virtue of tolerance, equality, and diversity through producers proud of their work, but only certain tolerances, equalities, and diversities.

Our values are not the masters of government and other authorities, but the servants. The nationalism, Christian conviction, and other self-belief that could have empowered us to resist other people's influence, no longer empower us. They no longer defend us.

Without families, races, and nations from which to draw strength and ground us, we are susceptible to corrupting circumstances: to the most powerful among us and to outsiders moulding our senses of right and wrong, filling us with ideologies that tribespeople acting naturally would eschew. Each ideology leaves us vulnerable to every next mounting ideology, neglecting if not harming us.

The masses of people simply follow. People deeply indoctrinated presume not only that they have not been indoctrinated, but that the people disagreeing with them must have been indoctrinated. If we are not estranged from everyone before we believe what we are told, then with the ideologies instilled in us, we become estranged.

Increasingly ideological and pervasive mass media, entertainment, and education mean each change along our road of suppressing and even eradicating human nature comes a little more rapidly than the last. Vulnerable to political construction, we are not shaped by the masses but by the lunacy of a few individuals.

Journalism

We nevertheless feel empowered. Our proudly empowered free public insists we do not trust journalists. We still wind up believing them.

When computer networks allowed the growth of dissident media, the mainstream media labelled the dissident news fake news. The dissident news may well have been factually correct, but it was ideologically incorrect, for what it evidenced.

Journalistic ethics once insisted upon reporting only the facts without personal opinions. They have come to focus upon personal opinions with only interest in the facts that affirm those opinions.

Facts at odds with those opinions are withheld from publication. Propaganda is not merely the inclusions, but the omissions.

Whether a story is factual is immaterial to whether propagandists say it, but the cleverest propaganda is factual. Propaganda becomes the stories and aspects of stories untold.

Those inconvenient facts might be deemed irrelevant. Facts supporting those personal opinions are relevant.

In this Age of Ideology, those inconvenient facts might simply be offensive or socially divisive. Allegations supporting those opinions are not.

Facts might be withheld for being unproven, although the burden to prove facts defying the prevailing ideology is much greater than the burden to prove allegations supporting that ideology. Allegations supporting that ideology need no evidence supporting them at all.

Our right of free speech has become the right not to speak: not to report or even mention matters we consider distasteful. Information is selective, shirking away from reality bits we do not like. Convinced we are individuals unanswerable to anyone or anything, we believe whatever keeps us apart.

The End of Truth

What is happening in the West is not happening simply with our ignorance. It is happening with our conviction in the truth of matters untrue.

Respecting reality is not an ideology. It is a rejection of ideology.

Ideologies are premised not upon fact and reason but upon emotions: most profoundly the yearning for something good in which to believe, when we no longer believe in our races and cultures. Facts can play havoc with emotions.

Ideologies being imposed without regard for facts and reason, there is no need to try to support them with facts and reason. There is simply the ideal repeated over and over, as if it were factual and reasonable.

Conversely, facts and reason are no reason to reject an ideology. If they were, then there would have been no call for the ideology in the first place.

In this Age of Ideology, ideology prevails over fact. Ideology prevails over reason.

Central to our Age of Ideology is not just the paramountcy we give ideas, rather than facts. It is also the insistence that something is true not for being based upon our knowledge of facts but for being decreed to be true: for being ideologically true.

Human authorities say what is true. Dissidents do not say what is true, especially if it really is true.

Instead of discovering the truth, we decide it. Something is true because human authorities say it is true. The truth is whatever people deem it to be, or are led to believe.

They can then claim that science, history, and anything else confirm it is true, without anyone needing to check. We trust whatever we are told is the history or science to support a belief without investigating that history or science. We are left ignorant and misinformed about historical and present-day fact, human biology and nature, and racial reality.

Errors in fact are not errors anymore, provided they are ideologically sound: for suggesting something we know to be true. We demand the right to be right.

Ideologies become self-fulfilling, if only in people's heads, but that is where ideas and ideologies rest. Ideology supplants reality.

No civilisation can be built upon anything but reality, but we individuals are not trying to build a civilisation, not really. We are simply saying and doing whatever we want to do.

Ideology becomes reality. Reality and human nature are dismissed for being deemed mere ideologies.

Without sense of a greater good or value in facts, truth and lies have become equal in the ideological West. It is more than luxury in lying, because lying presupposes people know their words are untrue. Instead, lies become truths and truths become lies. Honest people become liars.

Lying about facts has become a legitimate public policy tool, if it promotes something that is ideologically true. It need only serve public policy objectives. We have made lying not simply a right but an obligation, when it defends and promotes racial, cultural, and sexual diversity.

Heroes and villains are both liars, although heroes claim the mantle of higher truth behind their lies. We are left only with lies.

Most lies of Marxist communism also operate under Western individualism, but with an extra big lie under communism: communists pretend that a collective good motivates them. The primary difference between communism and individualism became the honesty of individualists to admit their self-interests.

Our postmodern West might all be a lie, our lives complete lies. It is so hard to know. We do not know what the secrets are.

It is one thing to be ignorant. It is much worse to be certain otherwise.

Little wonder, our children disbelieve us. We rebuke people who do not lie as we lie, but the compliments we give ourselves only make our lies more pervasive. We have lost all sense of the truth.

The End of Critical Analysis

We imagine our forebears living like sheep with their duties to God, King or Queen, and Empire or Country, but they could think and question. Having naïvely answered our leaders call to war in 1914, our forebears realised their blunder sooner than our leaders realised theirs. We followed our leaders into World War II when they left us with no better choice.

Arrogant as we are, the kindest words we can say of our forebears are that they did not know any better: that they would have been like us if they had known what we know. We grant them the presumption of ignorance.

Ideology shuts down our capacity to question. It leaves us mindlessly compliant with the loudest voices around.

We prefer a poetic philosophy for a single human species in harmony, but without the questioning once intrinsic to Western philosophies. We live for today, without learning from yesterday or thinking much about tomorrow.

Judgement is a rational assessment having regard to all available information. Judging people used to encompass punishing them if our judgements found them guilty, as criminal courts did, but judgement no longer needs to punish people for us to refuse it.

Our rejection of judgement about people and cultures is a rejection of not just critical analysis, but any analysis. Ideas might come to mind.

Believing so much we have been told, we stopped trying to learn because we decided we already know. We depend upon what we have heard and read, but the little we know need not affect what we fervently believe. We are trusting, certain of the sincerity of strangers. We do not know enough to question.

Besides, we are busy enough as it is. Our jobs, families, and football teams do not leave us time to examine the orthodoxies around us. We are sheep because being sheep is simpler than being shepherds, or defying the sheepdogs barking.

Schools

Children know little of the world, except as others describe it. So do most adults. Our potted lives are products of our times and places.

Western education, especially at the elite levels, was once premised upon our senses of developing and defending civilisation, namely Western Civilisation. Western schools used to teach students to think.

An education system predicated upon critical analysis asks questions instead of dictating every answer, challenges children to be specific with their platitudes and criticisms, and assesses students by their logic and reasoning instead of their points of view. It provides the facts and definitions to let people think, instead of abandoning facts and definitions. It imparts a wealth of ideas and welcomes any more.

When the West became consumed with ideology over biology, we came to believe that nothing is innate and everything is learnt. Thus everything can be taught.

That is not simply a rejection of human nature and instincts, as well as instincts according to race, gender, or anything else physical. It is a prioritisation of propaganda and of education as a tool of propaganda.

The purpose of education became political or economic, because the purpose of everything in our Age of Ideology is political or economic. Schools, universities, and workplaces became doctrinaire, confining themselves to their ideological lines, as increasingly have our infant preschools and childcare.

We are not feeding facts but decrees, especially decrees for diversity. In the choice between knowledge and ideology, we teach ideology. We call it knowledge.

The lies we agree with, we call education. The facts we dislike, we call propaganda.

The core mission of Western education systems is not education. It is indoctrination, as it is for other education systems, but our indoctrination erases human nature: tribalism and collective self-respect.

What we used to call indoctrination, we now call dealing with issues. Dealing with issues has come to mean finding reasons to advance one point of view and to reject all others.

The rote learning systems of Asia became ours, albeit with much less for us to learn. Education became a matter of compliance.

Education became inculcation very well done, with tireless repetition never seeming repetitive. For all the rights we boast in our supposedly free societies, our right is not to think as we choose to think but as we are taught to think.

It is close to impossible for speakers with whom the people who set school syllabuses disagree to be heard. Western schoolchildren do not grow up rejecting dissident viewpoints. They grow up unaware dissident viewpoints exist.

Those children become adults. As regards people, cultures, or anything else, whole generations of white people cannot critically analyse anything, having come of age without an original thought, at least about anything important. With ideologies down pat, we are not so good with ideas.

People from other races and schoolchildren outside the West also come of age without original thoughts and cannot critically analyse anything, but they are promoting themselves and their cultures. They are not degrading them. They are not abandoning them.

Universities

Before Western schools became factories for ideology, Western universities and colleges became factories. The most popular lecturers are those spoon-feeding students. We are not there to discover. We are there to be told. We are not there to think, but to learn.

For all our education, we become devotees of other people's thought, believing people calling themselves expert in their fields much as we expect to come to call ourselves experts in ours. Students are the marketplace, and we demand education without challenge: training for fools.

Our lives and careers depend upon us conforming to powerful people's opinions. We dare not question what they say. We do not even consider doing so.

We do not want to read facts or learn ideas that might adversely affect our subject results. We learn what we need to work and to spend.

What we call the intelligentsia is more a matter of profession and opinionated self-certainty than intelligence. Ideology supplanting intellect means relegating genii to the idiot masses if their politics veer from the norm.

We have politicised knowledge, interpreting facts to make conclusions keeping us in our careers. When ideology supplants scholarship, stupidity becomes scholastic.

Academics are as vulnerable as the rest of us to the politics of people and power. They need the esteem of universities and people passing through them, conferring government and other endowments.

The peer review process, which previously ensured academic papers were intellectually sound, now ensures they are politically correct. Academia compels academics to say certain things are true that they know to be false. Thus so do the students, for the rest of their lives.

Any field of study that might have defended or advanced Western Civilisation is no longer a matter for study, for people so indifferent if not hostile to that civilisation. It is a matter for uncompromised compliance, compelling us through our decline.

The End of Enlightenment

An invention of ancient Greece, democracy was predicated upon individuals with different ideas to express and arguments to expound. We assumed their expression and argument would reveal a common good.

Classic liberalism valued independent thought. It drove our Age of Enlightenment.

Europe's Age of Enlightenment remained an age of races, city-states, and nations, while encouraging individuality. With nationalism and other tribalism, we engaged with different points of view.

Our common identity did not depend upon our agreement upon anything, except that we had a common identity: our race and collective religion. Nationalism did not discourage people from thinking independently of each other. It facilitated it.

Nationalism was not conservative. With the confidence of nations in which we stood, we were emboldened to explore new ideas.

We accommodated something of each other's desires and personal interests in formulating public policy. We pursued a common good because we believed we were people in common. We compromised, for the sake of us all, without denying our desires.

The Age of Enlightenment was predicated upon people having different points of view in their common pursuit of the truth, whatever the truth happened to be. We wanted knowledge, whatever knowledge happened to be. We wanted facts, whatever the facts happened to be.

Ideologies reject alternate points of view, because ideologies do not pursue truth. They decide it.

Communism rejected everything Western. It rejected for being bourgeois the political and economic legacies of our Age of Enlightenment: classic liberalism and free market economics. Both were predicated upon people making choices and making different choices.

We of the free West condemn much of our past European practice and thought, but shy away from condemning those legacies. We simply fail to defend them.

If our Age of Enlightenment did not end with the Great War, it ended with the Holocaust. This Age of Ideology increasingly sets boundaries to thoughts, feelings, and beliefs beyond which we cannot transcend. For all our talk of the individual, we have lost our respect for independent thought, at least about any thought questioning or defying a prevailing ideology.

With ideology paramount, classic liberalism becomes obsolete, if not seditious. So does democracy.

Ideologues respect democracy only when people vote for the correct candidates and parties. Whereas people outside the West protest apparent election results they feel do not express the people's will, for reasons of fraud or the like, ideologues protest election results in the unnatural West that do reflect the people's will, because they disagree with the people.

Ideologues ride roughshod over those with whom they disagree, granting them nothing. Without a common identity and thus common good, there is no longer compromise between conflicting opinions.

Freedom of Speech

Through our Age of Enlightenment, we could think whatever we wanted to think. We could say whatever we wanted to say. We respected each other's right to speak, even if we did not listen.

Freedom of speech was not an ideology. It was a practical measure, which allowed us to correct our errors. The West developed and believed in freedom of speech because imperfect beings can err.

Reasonable people seeking truth can disagree. Scholars

deliberate upon propositions right or wrong, in the spirit with which they are made. Good ideas need air to germinate. Bad ideas need conversation to wither.

The freedom to disagree allowed us to critique, and to teach others the truth. Errors can be as useful as accuracies in learning the truth. People with whom we disagree can teach us more than people with whom we agree.

Free speech was only meaningful because it extended to all opinions, however unpopular, unpalatable, or apparently wrong. If reasonable people are wrong, they want to be told they are wrong, so they can learn. Reasonable people do not suffer if they hear something wrong, provided they feel free to disagree. Learning from each other, we all become wiser.

Freedom of speech was a means of pursuing truth, but ideologies insist they are the truth. We are no longer trying to learn; we have decided all we want people to know, or other people have decided for us. In this Age of Ideology, the West has stopped learning, about anything important.

The only free speech for an Age of Ideology is speech that conforms to a prevailing ideology, whatever that happens to be at a time and place. Our Western right of free speech is a right to agree and agree publicly, that is all. Classical freedom of speech, encompassing dissident viewpoints, has become free speech extremism.

The people most hostile to freedom of speech are those most in need of being told they are wrong. Our human authorities have become dominated by people who think that any person disagreeing with them is an idiot, or worse.

Our right of free speech has become the right of loud voices to drown out gentle speakers, whose right is to whisper so no one can hear. We cannot stop people shouting louder than we do, even if they are so busy shouting they do not pause to speak and do not care to listen. We have no right to be heard but a right to be ignored, if we are fortunate.

For all our talk of diversity, we have none of ideas and opinion, no intellectual plurality, not about anything important. Other ideas might be right, even brilliant, but nobody listens and nobody learns.

Offence

We presume our forebears were indoctrinated to think and feel as they did, but they had freedom to feel their natural feelings and to say what they thought to be true. They did not fear others virulently feeling offence.

To ignore what people say when we disagree with them would be true individualism. Instead, we are offended.

Feelings, the West wants. Truth, we have made less important.

No longer are we right for saying that is rational or factual. Instead, we are right for being offended.

Something becomes true because we feel good believing it. Something becomes false because we are offended. Our offence demonstrates our complete emotional immersion in a prevailing ideology.

Encountering different viewpoints becomes challenging for people never before encountering different viewpoints. People who insist something is true because it is said to be true, whatever the illogic and lack of evidence for that belief, do not suffer being challenged.

They might well be traumatised. With our ideological identity, there is nothing more traumatic than encountering a contrary idea, particularly if it is factually accurate.

Reality is immaterial to ideology. It can be offensive.

We do not examine our beliefs and what they imply, so do not want to hear other people critiquing them. We do not even clarify them.

Some people's feelings matter more than other people's feelings. Feelings of offence among people subscribing to a prevailing ideology matter far more than feelings of offence among people who do not subscribe. The feelings of the latter do not matter at all.

The wrong more than the right fear the facts. The foolish more than the wise restrict debate.

Offence is for fools. Few things threaten the unthinking more than a thought. Nothing threatens the unthinking more than a thought uttered aloud, particularly one uttered without conviction that it be true or false by a person thinking about it. Any twit can condemn a thought, some wisdom allows a person to rebuke it, but the greatest wisdom is required of the person who considers what is credible, whatever the outcome of that consideration.

Among people without religious or national offence to feel, there is no surer sign of a simple idea having become a cruel ideology than people shutting down discussion and debate about it. Ideologies are prisons in which to be trapped.

The Rule of Words

Simply because we abandoned rules of grammar and spelling does not mean the English language is without rules altogether. The unnatural West has abandoned notions of blasphemy and obscenity in respect of God and morality, but we enforce something much stricter advancing ideology.

New rules replaced them, enforced more harshly than mere grammar and spelling, even blasphemy and obscenity, ever were. Scrutinising what people say more than anything they do, words previously unimportant have become all-important, to people without anything innovative or profound to declare.

Our words do not have to be factually accurate or beautifully put together. They have to be ideologically correct.

The point of semantics is no longer to be clear in our communication, courteous, or elegant. It has become changing people's attitudes, including our own, in this Age of Ideology.

When powerful people demand children or adults say something, they demand we think it. Dictating our language dictates our thoughts, so that changing the words we use changes the way we think. Their words from our lips manipulate our minds to their particular points of view, when we say them often enough, and to having no view at all.

We believe in words without trying to understand them, however many times they are written up in lights. Language does not have to make sense anymore.

Words have come to mean so much because thoughts mean so much, but words are easier to hear and so police than are thoughts. We worry about every spoken word.

In our Age of Ideology, language has become a means to silence and oppress. We have let words become weapons.

SIMON LENNON

Political Correctness

Senselessly, we chant every ideological dictate around us, however irrelevant it might seem to the matter at hand. We thereby feel part of an ideological tribe, in which we vest our identity and confidence.

What is popularly called political correctness is really the imposition of ideology, involving every person in that enforcement every time we encounter another person. We might be powerless to resist in the words that we utter and thoughts that we hold, but we are powerful in imposing submission upon others.

Under communism, dissent was not seeing the success and truth of communism, connecting every person on earth together. Under individualism, dissent is not seeing the success and truth of individualism, separating us from each other.

Dissent might be an engagement with objective reality, when the ideologues declare reality to be something else. It might be logic and reason, when the ideologues are driven by edict and emotion. It might be re-engaging with races and religious traditions from which we have moved so far apart of late, ours and everyone else's. It might be retaining or finding anew the self-belief the rest of the West has lost.

Dissent is not discussed but is scornfully shut down. Ours are conflicts without conversation. Discussion, be damned.

At best, we treat anyone holding a dissident viewpoint as an ignorant fool, not to know what we know that everyone knows. We do not fail to persuade. We refuse to discuss.

We treat repeating political correctness a hundred times a day as if it were perfectly reasonable, but expressing dissent just once as if it were extremism. We treat expressing dissent twice as obsession.

At worst, however physically or mentally weak we might be, we can all bully dissidents into submission. We demonise dissidents, without distraction wasting time considering their words. Political correctness can be very empowering for people otherwise powerless and for people already powerful.

The force of the many prevails over the fragility of the one, however many ones there are. Fact, reason, and goodness are immaterial.

Dissent became bigotry, with all its implications of stupidity and nastiness. Bigoted against bigotry, the butts of our bigotry are the dissidents we label bigots, whatever they think they are.

Bigots are simply the people with whom we disagree. More venomous and uncompromising than other bigotries, the only people we are not treating as equal are people who disagree with us.

We live in an era where calling someone a bigot is considered persuasive argument, to an audience fearful of being called the same. Calling a person a bigot with expletives is considered oratory.

Postmodern Phobias

More pointedly, there are the postmodern phobias we accuse bigots and other dissidents of suffering. Phobias are irrational fears.

The dissident might not feel afraid, but so at ease have we become in our ideological mindset, we presume dissidents must be afraid, without us necessarily wondering what they must fear. This Age of Ideology presumes to decide not just what is true, but also what is fear.

Having decided we are rational, we are certain that people not sharing our views, and what we are certain are all rational people's views, must be irrational. Lumped among our ideological phobias are the most rational of fears, when those fears are of something that ideologically should not be feared.

So too are any attempts to examine rationally a matter the subject of our ideological dictates, for considering that there might be reason to examine it rationally. We accept every ideological dictate without question, so we think questioning our ideologies can only be irrational. Rationality is deemed to be irrational.

Paradoxically, there is nothing more irrational in our ideological West than the reflexive labelling of dissent as a fear and an irrational fear at that. Irrationality is deemed to be rational.

Our postmodern phobias are all anti-intellectual, shutting down free speech and thus rational thought. They are slanders to silence dissent.

Unwilling or unable to engage in rational discourse as we are, labelling people bigots or sick with a phobia makes them the issue. We are thus excused from justifying our viewpoints or rationally critiquing theirs. If they do not walk away, we will.

Hate Speech

When labelling bigots with a phobia is not enough, there is labelling their dissent as hate speech: another ideological invention devoid of reason. The only curse we loathe more than being accused of an irrational fear is being accused of hatred.

Insisting that ours are ideologies of love, we think that anybody defying our ideologies must be hateful. Thus dissent becomes hate speech, however much it arises from the dissident's love or desire for truth.

Telling the truth is hate speech, when reality defies what has been ideologically deemed to be true. The person accused of hate speech does not need to hate anyone or anything, but this Age of Ideology presumes to decide not just what is true and what is fear, but also what is hate.

Real love and facts are no excuse. Love is deemed to be hate.

Paradoxically again, there is no greater hatred in our ideological West than that coming from those shouting down dissent for supposedly being hate speech. What we call a campaign against hatred is not a campaign against hatred, because we hate people we accuse of being hateful. Hatred is deemed to be love.

Bigotries, phobias, and hate speech are normally just white people pursuing the truth or caring for our own, or even simply believing we have an own. Is it any wonder that people grow up unable to analyse critically when they see every questioning of the prevalent ideology prosecuted as hate speech?

We used to love each other and ourselves, we European peoples. Our love has slumped with each world war, waning still further since then.

There are more words taunting white people for what we supposedly fear or hate, than words we used to have for loving our own, like Anglophile. By the twenty-first century, words of loving Europe and Europeans have faded from use.

We love less than we used to love. We do not really love anything.

For all our self-righteousness, a monster in our body politic enjoys hating. Hating more than we used to hate, no hatred on earth is more vehement than the hatred that white people have come to feel for each other. Those who marshal that monster can mobilise the masses against anyone, even us, in the name of smashing such hatred. No other race is so inimical to its own, to anyone who would save it.

The Tyranny of Ideology

Bravery used to be fighting wars in our country's defence. In this Age of Ideology, bravery is being politically incorrect.

With ideologies ignited by the Great War debacle burning more fiercely than ever, the cruellest conflicts in the world became those between white people. Our tribal instincts no longer expressed through our races and nations became manifest in our opinions. We like or loathe people not for their actions, but for their thoughts, feelings, and beliefs: joining us in our subservience to ideologies.

Without races or collective religions connecting us with other people, ideologies at least offer commonality. We seek satisfaction in ideology, no matter how antithetical to tribalism that ideology might be. Mere commonality lacks the connectedness, loyalty, and morality of tribalism, but is still better than being mere individuals.

In the name of inclusion, we exclude people we deem to be not as inclusive as we are. The dissidents are not excluding people. The people demanding inclusion are excluding people. Inclusion becomes exclusion. Exclusion becomes inclusion.

This is the cancel culture, by which we cancel from our sight and hearing and from other people's sight and hearing anyone who dares disagree with us. Communists erased dissidents from old photographs. We ban their writings and artworks. We prohibit them from speaking.

When dissidents are no longer alive, we pull down their statues and rename anything that formerly bore their name, even if they paid for it. It becomes as if the person never was, as if that erases the act or viewpoint in dissent.

There never used to be mobs to rival the mobs of individuals driving us to our ideological norms, taking hold whenever anyone dissents. Joining is much safer than resisting the ideological mob, however absurd or fanciful the latest ideological dictate might be.

Submitting to the power of the many over the meekness of one, our ideological mobs are our ideological tribes. They give us some semblance of connectedness with the rest of our mob, feeling a little less of the psychological fragility to which individualism condemns us.

Mobs are hysterical in nature. Like ideologies, mobs are more for attacking others than defending their own. Mobs lack the comfort and contentment that families, nations, and races can offer.

Individuals are no less individuals for joining a mob, even if there are those among the mob who could be their people. They lose only their individuality.

Communists in power enjoyed and still enjoy police and gulags to enforce their ideologies. Never knowing who among them might inform upon dissidents to the police, people felt compelled to inform upon each other. They could not risk another person informing the police of an act or word of dissent but also mentioning other people who had seen that act or heard that word. Being aware of dissent without informing the police would make a person appear like a dissident too. So every citizen felt compelled to inform upon every other.

When Western police enforce the supposedly free West's rules of hate speech, we move ever closer to our ideological mentors: the Marxists. We are so proud of our libertarian visions we cannot see our new totalitarianism: the tyranny of ideology, including the tyranny not just of communism but also of individualism.

We torment, ostracise, and frighten dissidents, until dissent disappears. It is the death of discussion.

The language of liberties does not match the practice. Without nationalism or other tribalism to defend us and our freedoms, the unnatural West became subject to ideological totalitarianism.

Totalitarianism does not require totalitarian government, because regimes can be much more than government. The greatest infringement upon liberties is the liberty to oppress.

Self-Censorship

Few of us suffer to say words that powerful people do not want to hear, even if those powerful people are no more than acquaintances and other strangers upon whose earshot we walk. With few people with whom to confide, we have little extent to speak freely.

Much as East Europeans did through their decades under communism, we learn to say and to write what we must. We slavishly or self-interestedly follow the loudest forces around, knowing life is easier if we comply.

Shouting each other down means we cannot hear our whispers. We hide in our skin hoping nobody knows our secret-most thoughts; a voice is not a voice if no one can hear. We pretend so much, but demonise anyone who suggests we are pretending.

Perhaps, saying what a person does not believe lulls him into believing. Affirmations might lull her into not believing anything.

People who have stopped believing their own words are no longer certain that other people believe theirs. It is easier not to think.

When all other censorship is in place, the last is self-censorship inside people's heads. Rather than suffering the aggravation of other people censoring our spoken or written words, we do not consider what we have learnt we are forbidden to say or to write.

People who believe what we ought to believe are most likely to say what we ought to say. People who question and speak aloud of their questions will almost certainly utter them wrongly.

We have lost our chance for undisciplined thoughts. If we are not careful, we might think.

Without freedom of speech, we have lost freedom of thought, and freedom to feel. Our right is to believe what others want us to believe and to feel what others want us to feel. The most complete censorship is within people's souls.

When people insist we believe what they want us to believe, even reward us for believing what they want us to believe, we believe, or at least pretend to believe. Sincerity remains profoundly important. We have to learn how to fake it.

Individualism without Individuality

Ours is not just the individualism we make for ourselves. It is the individualism to which others confine us.

In the atmosphere of increasingly individual self-interest, we have no reason to be anything better. Sensible people find reason to change, to become no less individualistic than are the people around them. Only fools persist with tribal identities when men and women who could have been their tribespeople persist with being mere individuals. People weary of their treatment by individually interested others become individually interested too. Time would come to admire and long for the fools.

Individualism is infectious. Individualism begets individualism.

Isolation does not breed uniqueness. A great paradox of Western individualism has been that it pushes aside individuality. We individuals became more alike.

Individualism breeds conformity. Ideology demands it.

Nationalism, racism, and other tribalism bred individuality, in the West. They are no longer the norm.

What had been a myriad of countries and cultures has become the almost uniform West. We have become solitary swimmers in seas of our stolid sameness: an incredible likeness of being.

We never noticed ideological individualism replace individuality. Transfixed with both, we have lost sight of how much we are like other white people. We have become too insular to notice how much other white people are like each other.

Ours remains a uniquely Western vision, condemning each of us to being individuals alone. Other races are not the individuals we are, not all the time. They retain their tribes, races, and nations as we had, just a few generations ago.

Having rejected race out of hand, white people do not realise how different we are from other races. We cannot recognise Western phenomena. We cannot see how strange we have become.

Tribalism

Tribalism takes us beyond the people we know to people we do not. When we enjoyed our biological tribes, we did not need any more tribes. Without our natural tribes, ours are whatever unnatural tribes we can find.

With our individual rights, our post-racial post-national tribes are those to which we choose to belong, up to a point. Existing tribe members with their individual rights are not obliged to admit us.

Tribes are not open to newcomers, not immediately anyway. If they are not slow to accept newcomers, they are not really tribes.

To satisfy and inspire us, tribes cannot be merely schooling, sporting, or geographical coincidence. They are not the dictate of government edict, bureaucratic plan, or court ruling. They do not need exhorting by company human resources or marketing departments. They do not require slogans, advertising campaigns, or (worst of all) laws and ethics. They do not depend upon ties, lapel pins, or flags, however stirring those symbols might be. They do not rely upon anthems or songs, however rousing some are.

To be a tribe we need tribespeople thinking as a tribe; that is all. Every other thought and desire can be unique to each man or woman, boy or girl, but for that sense of comprising a tribe. Tribes are the people on our side as much as we are on theirs, not because we are compelled to be but because we are allowed to be. They are tribes in which we believe without being told to believe.

With tribalism, we are slow to let go of relationships. Free to argue because arguing is relationship without risk of separation, tribesmen and women support each other without ego or constraint. In a contest between individual interests, individual interests normally prevail, but the self-interest is that of the group. Tribalism is a reason to treat fellow tribesmen and women well, for the good of the tribe.

Instead of asserting any poor individualism, tribalism allows us to indulge our rich individuality. Without individualism, we have individuality.

The only multiplicities of tribes in which people can stand are concentric: tribes within tribes. People cannot be part of two or more tribes whose members exclude each other.

For there to be a common good, there must be something common. If we are to believe in a good greater than each of us, then we need to believe there is something greater than each of us: something outside our individual selves to consider. Tribal good requires tribes, such as families, races, and nations.

Communists thought they could create something common with their multiracial secular collectivism: something greater than each individual other than biological or religious tribalism. They could not. At least they tried.

The End of Loyalty

Tribalism encompasses many feelings and values. Among them is loyalty. Intrinsic to loyalty and allegiance is that we distinguish a person or group of people to whom we are loyal from those to whom we are not.

Individuals do not distinguish between people. We call it discrimination.

Tribes are innately discriminatory. Tribespeople discriminate in favour of their fellow tribespeople above others. Fellow tribespeople reciprocate.

Loyalty is discrimination. Loyalty to our family includes nepotism. Loyalty to our country is nationalism. Loyalty to our race is racism.

Without discrimination, Western individualism leaves no room for loyalty to anyone. We no longer give loyalty, nor expect to receive it. We treat disloyalty to our own as a virtue.

Loyalty would impinge upon our powers to pick and choose whomever and whatever we want, for whatever self-centred or self-righteous reasons we want. We demand our individual rights too much to let loyalty affect us, without appreciating how much we lose by not enjoying loyalty from others.

No less than our right to disloyalty is our right to demand loyalty from others, but we have learnt that our compatriots are no more loyal to us then we are to them. Subordinates whom we have no right to command offer only a semblance of obedience, if that.

There is never real camaraderie among any group in our unnatural West. The best we grant is the best we hope to receive: that for a time it suits each of our individual interests to ally ourselves together. Our alliances are temporary convergences, lasting to whatever extent and for as long as it suits us and suits others.

Whenever three or more people gather, there are politics. No people are more political than individualists. Unfettered by morality, loyalty, or genuine relationships, individual interests compel them to adopt every technique to advance their individual selves. They ally ourselves with people they think might be of assistance, for as long as they think it.

All we post-racial post-national individuals have are whatever small relationships we steal for ourselves: private matters between private individuals, transient compilations of solitary self-interests. We have become solitary strangers, staying together for as long as it suits us and others to do so.

Instead of friends, we hire professional counsellors who do as they are told, without difficult vagaries or unpleasant compromise. Unlike friends, they remain, for as long as somebody pays: the best of friends.

Friends are for people who do not have careers. Friends for people who do have careers are consultants. Our friends are the people we trust enough to appoint to a job rather than people we have already appointed; few people at work become friends.

Friends are not friends in our unnatural West. They are income opportunities.

We favour friends over strangers, but when individual interests are at stake, friendships mean little. When the skies become dark, we are no more loyal to our friends than to anyone else.

Money measures everything. Friends betray friends.

We have not so much friends as networks: moments of coincident individual interests. If we are allies then we are allies up to the point of our respective individual interests: alliance without allegiance.

Financial friendships are all that we have. All money accords us are commercial acquaintances: relationships without relationship. Without financial foundations, without further financial reasons to befriend us, they are not friendships at all.

The End of Empathy

Like loyalty, empathy does not exist in abstract. It is felt for specific people or groups of people.

Empathy requires tribalism of some form. Where clans and other tribalism prevail, people only empathise with others from their clan or tribe, if anyone.

Tribespeople feel each other's feelings. They share their suffering.

Without community or other tribalism, we lost connectedness with other people. We have lost the genesis for empathy: a common identity. We lost our empathy.

However much we might champion other races' interests, people do not empathise with people from other races. People naturally empathise only with people from their race, if anyone.

With empathy comes altruism, even heroism. Within a family,

tribe, or race there can be heroism. Without empathy, we have lost much of our altruism, at least for each other.

Without empathy and altruism, people's actions can nevertheless aid other people, often people from other races and nations, but aiding those other people is less of a motivation than are their precious feelings about themselves and other self-interests. They will fob off the harm they do a million people to laud themselves for any benefit they do one person, or think they do one person.

If there is a characteristic common to ideologues, it is their lack of empathy for others: their disregard for the impact of their ideologies upon others. They might accuse their critics of a lack of empathy, because they know empathy is a virtue and the accusation will press their critics into submission. They often claim empathy among their many supposed virtues, but people with empathy would have regard for the consequences of their actions and ideals upon others.

Trying to inculcate unnatural empathies for people of other tribes and races, we lose our natural empathies. If tribalism leaves people without empathy for people of other tribes, then communism, individualism, and other globalism produce people without empathy for anyone.

Individualism ended Western empathy. What were our nations have become arrays of individuals indifferent to each other. Western individuals do not feel each other's pain: sociopathy.

Morality and Conscience

Morality arose naturally among tribespeople caring for their tribe, empathising with each other. Their common identity implied a common good and intrinsically each person's good. Collective identities protected and defended tribespeople, most of all from each other.

Morals expressed the principles by which people helped and protected each other. They were obligations to others, primarily if not only others within a community, nation, and race. Morals compelled and curtailed us in order to safeguard others, as they compelled and curtailed others in order to safeguard us.

Morality deemed something right for being good for the

community, country, and people within them. Morality deemed something bad because it harmed a community, country, and people within them, especially the most vulnerable among those people. Morality flowed from people's connectedness with each other: their nationalism or other tribalism.

Unnatural feelings are unlikely to be good. Natural feelings might not always be good, but morals prevent people from acting upon their natural feelings in circumstances harming themselves, their families, or their communities. Forbidding us from fulfilling unfortunate facets of human nature for the sake of our societies, families, and selves does not mean denying our nature, but acknowledging it.

Tribes innately developed and declared what was morally right and wrong. Religion might seem to have declared what was morally right and wrong, but generally religious morals codified conclusions of past generations.

Races differ, to a point. Thus morality is cultural, in part.

Morality can vary between tribes according to their different senses of the common good, in the circumstances in which they survive, although most morals proved universal. Ancient tribespeople all considered stealing from people within their tribe to be morally wrong, even if they had no qualms about stealing from people outside their tribe.

People retaining a sense of morality could still fall short of it. While other races knew only the force of law and other external compulsion enforcing their rules of behaviour, ancient Greece developed the Western concept of a conscience. A conscience is an inner sense enforcing our moral obligations, irrespective of what other people notice. Other races did not have a sense of a conscience any more than a sense of soul.

The End of Morality

The only enduring motivation inspiring people around the world to be good to each other has proven to be tribalism of some form or another, such as racism, nationalism, or collective religion; some races, nations, and religions anyway. Tribespeople may well mistreat people from outside their tribe, some tribes on earth more so than others. Individuals are free to maltreat everyone, particularly their own. We can steal from anyone.

Erasing our national and racial lines erased our morality. The more individualistic the West has become, the more estranged from our senses of race and family, the more immoral we have become.

Individualism is intrinsically incompatible with morality. There is no tribal interest among individuals. There is only individual self-interest. Thus without society or other tribalism, there is no morality. We have no sense of our society being harmed because we have no sense of our society.

We have lost the geneses for morality: tribalism and empathy. Without tribalism, there is no empathy. Without empathy, there is no morality.

Western individualism ended Western morality. We will not find morality in isolation.

Ideological and other political correctness are not morality. They are self-righteousness wielded to intimidate others.

Without tribalism, not even Christianity compels much morality. Individualism strips morality from Western Christianity.

We presume so much goodness in people without tribalism, but a conscience depends upon connectedness. A conscience cannot form in isolation.

Being individuals with individual rights, we cannot comprehend a conscience to constrain us, for that would contradict the rights on which we predicate life. How could a mind contain within it a conscience that restricts the mind's right to choose what it wants? Each person can only have one individual interest. So, we reason, there is no such creature as conscience. At least, we would reason as much, if we ever considered it.

Without morality, what remains are rights, such as the right to self-harm and the rights we give strangers to harm our compatriots. Rights reflect our refusal to help each other, and our excusing of others from helping us.

We do not care who we hurt. Other people care no more about hurting us than we care about hurting them.

The end of society is the end of morality. The end of morality is the end of civilisation. The end of society is the end of civilisation.

Personal Morality

Individualism denies any objective morality among a race or other tribe because it refuses to recognise races and other biological tribes. Individualism makes morality subjective, not simply for varying between different cultures but for varying between different individuals. Each person decides for himself or herself what his or her morals should be, without God or society dictating them.

Among the choices individuals make is whether to make the morals of a religion theirs. Without tribalism and with Christianity optional, morality became optional.

Morality in the unnatural West became an individual private matter: the very antithesis of the collective good that grounded collective morality. She has the right to decide her own values. He is true to himself. She will find her own way.

Lo and behold, individuals each declare moralities by which we are good for doing what we want to do anyway. Something became right because we demand the freedom to do whatever we like, without anyone saying we should not. We profess moralities without regard for the impact upon others, or even ourselves.

Immorality would be doing what we do not want to do anyway, or we know we will later regret. Badness would also be what we do not want other people to do.

People do not choose moral responsibilities that would constrain or compel them. They choose moral responsibilities to constrain or compel others. Those others do the same.

Free market morality is whatever individuals want it to be, which makes morals meaningless. Any claim to morality formed in isolation is more individualism.

Each self-serving individual considers himself morally upright. Other people are good when they accede to her. They are bad when they do not.

With tribalism and thus morality, the premise of right and wrong was people looking after each other, or at least trying to do so. Without tribalism, the premise of right and wrong is people leaving each other alone.

Duty and Honour

With nationalism and other tribalism came duties to our families, nations, and races. The details of our duties depended upon our respective capacities and upon the circumstances.

Duty was the converse to morality. If morality was a constraint upon our actions, then duty was an obligation to act.

With duty came honour, our primary reason for complying with our duties. Honour was to duty what conscience was to morality, except that honour was not unique to Europeans. Other civilisations also understood honour, if only among men. Honour differed between races because duties differed between races.

Among Europeans, honour lay primarily in our eyes and minds, where conscience lay. Among other civilisations, honour lay primarily in other people's eyes and minds.

In Europe, women had honour too, but their honour was also the duty of men to protect. Men might have been more likely to talk of their duty than women (aside from the finest royalty and noblewomen) talked of their duty, but women knew their duties to their families and nations well enough. Their husbands and sons knew their duties to their families and nations too, and thus their duties to them.

Every duty we owed our children, our parents once owed us. Every duty we owed our parents, our children would owe us.

We reciprocated one by honouring the other. Tribalism had practical benefits.

Duties were greatest upon those most able to provide: the strongest, healthiest, and richest. They were least upon those least able to provide, such as the very young and very old. We helped when we were physically and financially most able to help. We obtained help when we physically and financially most needed help.

Every duty we owed our elders, our juniors would owe us. Every duty we owed our ancestors, our descendants would owe us.

For sharing our tribes and nations, our duties to our compatriots were as much their duties to us. We did not question our responsibilities to our fellow citizenry because they had the same responsibilities to us. We helped each other.

Christianity also accorded us duties unto God and the risk of His judgement. God had no duties to us but in Him, we had trust.

The End of Duty

Duty led our men to fight and die in war on our behalf. When the Great War erased our self-belief, it erased our confidence in duty. When World War II frightened us from wanting self-belief again, it frightened us from feeling duty anymore.

Abandoning racism and nationalism might have added to Western feelings of obligation towards other races, but it ended feelings of duty towards our race. We no longer feel duty to our families and compatriots. They no longer feel duties towards us.

Individualism is intrinsically incompatible with duty. The end of society is the end of duty. The end of morality is the end of duty.

Without nationalism and other tribalism come not duties but demands. We cannot imagine owing duties to others, but demand so much from others, theirs are effectively duties to us.

Others disregard their supposed duties to us, unless the money we pay them or our other power compels them. We disregard our supposed duties to others, unless the money they pay us or their other power compels us.

Without morality, there are no moral duties, no moral obligations. The only duties are commercial and legal, however little or much that is worth.

Religions might theoretically compel us to duties unto God or to a god or the gods in which we believe. In practice, without tribalism of some form, we dictate the terms of our religion so as impose more duties upon others than upon us, and even more upon God, our god, or our gods than upon us.

Other races retain their tribalism. They retain their morality and any sense of duty, but only for their own.

When we are strong we do not have to worry, but we will not always be strong. When we are weak, the only help we will be able to get will be help we can buy. We can have dined where kings have dined, but the waiters will not care.

Traditional Rights

Without necessarily thinking of them as being rights, rights are normally collective: of a tribe, nation, or race, defending its territory, safeguarding its society. They are the converse of the moral obligations that tribespeople and compatriots feel to each other and to the group.

The West established individual rights too: economic, social, political, and other liberties carefully enunciated and documented. Personal rights were a concept making sense only to European races, with our sense that people were individuals as well as members of a state, nation, or race.

Individual rights remained inextricably linked to our collective rights: rights of a people of whom we were part. The rights that English barons forged in the Magna Carta of 1215 were for them, not others. Theirs were individual rights defying monarchial self-interest, albeit to other English people's benefit too.

Such rights were not merely the practicalities of people doing what they were physically and intellectually capable of doing. They relied upon national or local laws granting and safeguarding the exercise of those capabilities: rights at law.

Personal rights were powers that people earned or had conferred upon them by human authorities, most obviously monarchs and governments. They were primarily rights protecting them from those human authorities.

Reflecting Christian theology of human free will and seizing upon a British philosophical tradition, Thomas Jefferson wrote in 1776 that God, our Creator, granted people (meaning white people) inalienable rights: the rights of man, and woman. Nevertheless, rights remained a peculiarly Western perspective. When America called herself the land of the free, Americans understood theirs were American freedoms, not available elsewhere.

Those rights we called inalienable were not quite inalienable. We forfeited our liberties and even our lives if we wronged our societies. Individual rights remained meshed with our moral obligations to each other and with our duties to God and Country.

Post-National Rights

When the West gave up our cultural heritage and Christian conviction, we lost our rationales for rights, but retained the rights. The unnatural West does not recognise God endowing us with rights, without us wondering who or what might endow us. Our freedoms became rights we imagine existing naturally, innately to everyone: the rights of person, every person.

Our freedoms stopped being something we needed to earn and defend. Wars were for that, but we do not want wars anymore.

When our individual rights come into conflict with our retreating collective rights, individual rights prevail. No longer do free people fetter our rights with responsibilities to God or each other. We just want the rights, particularly our own.

Our rights are more than just laws or those granted to us by old documents, in a list set out one after another. In our conviction of freedom, our culture of rights, they have become an ambit sense of our natural entitlement: rights to do everything. In our lives without tribes, everything is within our individual rights. If we are not able to do something, then we ought to be.

Rights once protected people from their monarchs and governments. In our sense of entitlement, they are for governments to step in and provide. Rights are only rights if someone else pays for them.

No longer simply protections from monarchs and governments, our rights are also rights against our fellow citizens. If we still believe in God, the Creator, they are rights against Him.

We presume rights are all that we need, but ours give us no reason to feel fortunate or privileged because we expect them. We do not appreciate what we expect, and we expect everything. Nor do we necessarily enjoy them.

Other People's Rights

The problem with rights is not our rights, but other people's rights. Ours is the Age of Entitlement, but only for us. Our compatriots have no such entitlement, not when they impinge upon us.

Without moral restraint, individual rights pit each individual against other individuals at the best of times: one person's freedom against another person's freedom. Other people's rights never offend us more than when they fetter our rights. One person's rights are another person's impositions, but we do not suffer anything we do not have to suffer.

Some rights are more fundamental than others. Our rights are the most fundamental of all.

More than a right to be selfish, we expect to be. In prioritising our interests, we are the first and the last.

Our passion for freedom and free enterprise is for our freedom and free enterprise. We tolerate the rights of others and might even support them, unless we disagree with them. The corollary to insisting "*I* have the right!" is demanding to know, "What gives *you* the right?"

Nobody answers the question. We are too self-assured in our rights to respond, and too self-absorbed to bother.

Interestingly, nobody asks, "*Who* gives you the right?" We do not appreciate that people have rights because other people, be they in government, courts, bureaucracy, or the military, gave us or defended those rights, in the present or in the past. Rights are costly to create and enforce.

"*What* gives you the right" assumes rights come from some abstract construction of the universe: a natural order, wholly unrelated to whether we believe in God, a Creator. In the unnatural order the unnatural West contrives in place of any natural order, our compatriots' rights are not as inalienable as ours.

With rights and choice there is one person's power and another person's powerlessness. Without collective identities to inhibit us, rights empower people already powerful. Rights mean most to people rich enough to exercise them.

The rest have rights, but not opportunities. Rights empower the cruel at the expense of the kind.

Rights without Obligations

With nationalism and other tribalism, there came rights and obligations. With individualism, come only the rights.

Walking hand in hand with our right to commit is our right to breach our commitments. We do not breach undertakings to other people because, in our minds, we do not make them. Obligations would fetter individual rights, so we cannot conceive them. To make real commitment to anyone would diminish our much-vaunted rights, empowering the person or people to whom the commitment is made. We insist on being free to change our free minds.

Contracts without enforcement become merely guidelines. They are factors for us to consider in exercising our rights. They might affect us, but do not bind us. We do not do anything we do not want to do. We do not do anything we do not have to do, unless doing so is in our individual interest.

The unnatural West became so litigious not because we are determined to exercise our legal rights, but because the only way to compel others to honour their legal obligations to us is for us to be ready to sue them. What people hate most about lawyers is that lawyers stand up for the rights of others that people prefer to ignore.

The lawyers we want are our own. Wherever prospective plaintiffs are likely to sue, the time, cost, and trouble of court can make honouring the law (or at least appearing to honour the law) in the prospective defendant's interest. If complainants do not sue, it is because suing is not worth the time, cost, and trouble, or we are waiting until it is.

What matters are not the rights but the obligations of others, at least to us. Rights without the will and capacity to enforce them are not rights. They are indulgences.

The worst way that people could treat us would be the way we treat them, or would treat them, if it ever comes about. No one assists or consoles us, except for a fee. Other people do not respect our rights unless doing so is in their interests. We do not feel obligations to our compatriots, who in turn do not feel them to us.

We do not care if people dislike us, if those people cannot or will not inflict harm upon us. Only towards people we perceive having the capacity to affect us do we moderate our actions. We need to be careful whom we cross. Our self-interest requires it.

The Reality of Rights

Post-Christian rights are absolute, we insist: truly inalienable. Rights free us for our misdemeanours.

The reality of rights is unlike the theory. The more we affirm our individualism and assert our individual rights, the less likeable and pleasant a people we are. We think we are friendly because we compare ourselves to the worst people we know.

With the bad enjoying the same rights as the good, we have no reason to be good. With the horrid living better than the good, people are horrid. We have the right to be horrible.

Without thought of a tribe or society that might suffer loss, we have the right to commit victimless crimes. In determining what crimes or other wrongdoings are victimless, we look only for individual victims, without looking too hard to find them.

Our disparate unnatural West makes many crimes so impersonal they become victimless. Rather than admit that we are willing to hurt anyone to get what we want, we deny that we are hurting anyone at all.

We are not bad people for what we are doing. We are just going about our new Western lives, furthering our individual interests. We are being free, and free individuals to boot.

Other individuals cherish their interests and rights to choose, just as we do. It can be hard for people who mean well to think beyond rights we are tirelessly told are personal.

There need be nothing malicious in people pursuing all that they know, unconcerned and unaware what other people do. Those other people do not have to be trying to affect us. They need not notice us at all. People fall prey to other people's individual interests deliberately and inadvertently.

If our flaws lie not in our freedoms, they lie in our exclusion of everything else. Without nationalist or Christian restraint and compassion, we have lost checks and balances upon personal liberties. Our first instinct is we can do what we like. We can have whatever we want. Neither God nor a people moderate us; our individual interests lose compromise and compunction. No one tells *us* what to do.

So comprehensively inalienable are we convinced are our single-person rights, they remain however revolting we become. Nothing we might do will diminish them. We could wilfully annihilate all life and matter in the universe laughing merrily as we go, but in our last gasps through the ether, demand our individual rights.

Commerce

Karl Marx considered the races most capable of contributing to civilisation to be European, although he wanted us to leave our cultures and the rest of Western Civilisation behind for the sake of industrial and agricultural production, much as Marx's father had left his Jewish cultural heritage behind to continue working as a lawyer in Prussia. The West would come to do the same.

With Europe so deeply weakened, the Great War made America a major power, but it also diminished her sense of civilisation because her sense of civilisation had been grounded in Europe. By 1925, the chief business of the American people was business, said President Calvin Coolidge. It set the West along a trajectory by which, with every diminution of our racial and cultural self-belief through the twentieth century, economic activity increasingly consumed us.

With their races, nations, and cultures, our European forebears explored the world to gain knowledge, conquer wilderness, and bring civilisation. Our new vows are none of those motivations. They are to carry on business.

When we lost our racial identities, we lost our sense of being part of a collective religion and other culture. Without nation or race, we have no culture to call our own.

Only economics and politics remain; they are all we empty vassals have. This Age of Ideology brings politics and economics to the fore. When ours is not the Age of Ideology, it is the Age of Money, without morality holding anyone back. When all else has gone, all we have are things to buy and believe.

Instead of economics and politics being left to the edges of life, serving that life, they have become fundamental, as much under Western individualism as they were under communism. Without races and nations, economic and political interests become our only interests. Politics and economics supplant the cultures that ideologies do not expressly erase.

Concentrating on commerce, businesses do more than pay our wages and salaries; with vocation comes money and much more besides. They set our tasks and objectives; we measure success and failure by how well we do within them. They command so much of our thought.

People tending their street stalls might shudder to think they are like big company employees in swish city offices, but they can be no less the product of business and marketing. All that matters is the primacy they give working and spending.

The free markets that succeeded as a system for economics became a system for life. The world is commerce and consumption. Only work can fulfil. Only consumption brings reward.

We become forever more serious, less interesting, ignorant of the ideology that came to envelop us. We have no more call nor thought to dream, but only to work, want, and buy.

Corporations as Countries

If our famous old companies were like countries, they were countries of countries: mechanisms by which families, races, and countries, even empires, carried on business. Without races or countries, only the companies, firms, and other businesses remain.

Nationalism was reason to consider countries our home. In our unnatural West still wanting a home, companies are the best offer around.

Corporations became our surrogate countries: microcosms of whatever countries can be, and a little like our countries were. Among many suppliers and ever more customers and clients we hope, only one company needs to enclose us.

We might call Western corporations operating across many countries multinational but, like the unnatural West, they are more post-national, operating apart from countries. They can comprise offices in countries around the world, but countries and the world do not come into it. There are only companies.

Corporations offer us territory. The less our minds dwell upon our countries, the more they dwell upon our places of work. Second, perhaps, to our houses, apartments, or single-room sitters, our office interiors, workstations, and other workspaces became the paltry areas we have a chance to define. They are not very much.

Like countries, corporations are the people, or at least some of the people, residing in them. Without countries, corporations took up some of the structures and systems that peoples developed over hundreds and thousands of years. They reflect something innate to human beings we cannot discard or cannot discard us.

Corporations as Tribes

Companies were the last opportunities many white people enjoyed to form tribes: the people we think we might need, if we need people at all. Tribesmen and women can wear suits, slacks, and skirts, made of grass or not.

When companies were tribal, managers recruited people with whom they felt comfortable, as well for being good at their jobs. Comfort was predicated upon a sense of relationship, or at least the potential for one. Employees were not recruited for their values or any ideological crusade for diversity. They were not unmarried people chosen so they could work beyond customary business hours, although employees worked long hours if circumstances required it.

Employees fitted in well with each other. We joked and were rude about people not there, and sometimes about people who were. We talked of families and religion. We argued. Politics was a principal point of conversation. With personalities, passion, even emotion, there could be internecine conflict, as we have developed a lot since becoming individuals.

Employees conformed by the clothes that we wore and language we used, but they did not matter too much. We were not there to comply, although we followed instructions. Those instructions were good for the tribe and the business, and not to anyone's harm or expense. Organisations cannot function without people following instructions.

Employees did not need democracy to be tribal and might even have been more tribal without it, provided their leaders thought in terms of the tribe. Dictatorship can be benevolent.

Of all forms of nationhood, the most obvious that companies could not replicate was democracy. With the changes Western governments came to make to their countries against their citizens' wishes, Western countries ceased replicating it too.

When our only tribes were our jobs and our workplaces the only places we belonged, we could walk through city streets feeling estranged from the world merely for being unemployed, as we had not when we enjoyed nationalism and collective religion. People living in large cities expect not to see each other again.

Commercial Culture

Without countries and races, companies became the cultures we possess. Our only cultures are corporate cultures, but there is little to them. There is even less to them away from work.

Culture embraces creativity, but ours is commercial creativity. Western culture is a commercial culture.

With dedicated roles and specialisation, creativity and imagination serve commercial objectives. They are something for profit, psychology for selling, and innovation for new product lines: the province of marketers and advertisers in realms of deep people teams. They are something to buy in a gift for someone who had not imagined such a gift.

Corporations are no places for dreamers, unless the company business is selling those dreams. Consumers buy the dreams we want.

Business language focuses upon the task at hand, without distractions of emotion or colour. Quotation marks imagine people saying the words ascribed to them in media releases they never really said. Computer-scanned signatures imagine them signing reports they did not write.

Dulling language is easy with plagiarism. Words drafted as literature would not survive their first executive review, let alone reach the chairman. Not only are company directors uninterested in frivolity, they are unwilling to seem different to other directors. Our compositions avoid anything personal.

Businesspeople nevertheless adopt what they think is any new word to connote sophistication and science, provided the term does not sound too scientific as to be alien. We follow fads wherever we can.

Complicated niche words, if they can be called words, have become commonplace. Most industries, professions, and even some companies create their own clumsy language of commerce: industry-speak; business-speak. The more complicated the words the better, because the less likely it will be that people from other industries, professions, and companies can understand them.

Executives and ambitious employees buy books concerned with their work, especially books that compliment people they know or compliment companies for which they have worked. If they never read them, the books sit on their office shelves so people think that they have read them. If they have read them, they hide the books at their homes so people do not know that they have read them.

Instead of imparting the wisdom of age and experience, as we did when we had peoples and nations we wanted to aid, autobiographies by people still in their careers tend to be self-promoting. Those by people retired from their careers tend to be self-justifying.

Something creative in our Western minds remains unsatisfied by our postmodern fixation with spending and work. For many, creativity's last expression is devising names for new companies and code names for company and government projects.

We became less and less representative of our people and nations, and less and less imaginative. Company names that once would have been those of families operating them increasingly became acronyms, without hint of families or people at all.

The End of Corporatism

If our corporations replicated what our nations had been, where buildings were territories and guards in foyers secured borders, not much needed to change, but the individualism that replaced nationalism left no room for corporatism, even if the unnatural West has not come to associate corporations with quite as much killing as we have come to associate nations. If the only tribes left for the unnatural West are companies, then we have come to have no tribes at all.

What remains of corporations are, at their best, more like private clubs. When we had communities, employees liked working close together, but not anymore. Nothing does more to spoil relations between staff than being foisted in close proximity to each other.

The risk of individual accountability means the safest conduct is agreeing with everyone else. Our freedoms are the freedoms to join herds of opinion, charging one way and then another, however they are led. Mobs give us sanctuary. If everyone is wrong, then nobody is.

Directors normally exude a consensus absolving each of them from blame. Among executives, chief executives devolve accountability for their decisions from one person to none.

The corporate politic is somewhere to hide, whenever accountability threatens to harm us. A corpus will matters more than individual views, when it excuses us from implying opinions are ours. In talking and writing, people use the passive voice to dwell upon outcomes and avoid ascribing responsibility to anyone. We become lost among others, hoping to escape blame for the blunders.

Even when asserting our self-interests through a group, we maintain our isolation as a birthright. We might speak of a group, without letting the group diminish our individual interests. Individual interests diminish the group.

Whatever powerful people decide, we all decide. When they blunder, they punish others.

Few skills are more important to good management than finding external causes of failure. Success is all our doing, failure not ours at all.

We have the right to sheet home the blame upon others whenever anything goes wrong. Those others too have the right, although we do not respect it, to sheet home the blame for all failures back on us.

Failure can be a reason to learn, instead of to quit. The best failures are those for which we suffer no harm and are not held accountable, but from which we can learn. Other people's failures, for which we are held accountable, are the failures hardest to bear.

Companies can be killing fields. Firing people is the easiest way to impose authority over people left behind.

Our post-national careers pursue neither prosperous empires nor even countries to command, but companies small enough to control; the smaller the company, the smaller the people. The most individually self-centred ambition is the most absolute.

Commercial Aristocracies

We without races and nations have become ever more stratified, with each stratum pursuing strata above uninterested in strata below. Without racism or nationalism, we slowly stopped expecting people more senior than us to act in our interests, unless it happens to be in their interests too. Sectional interests replaced racial and national interests.

The new Western aristocracies are not premised upon the favours of monarchs or generations of blue-blooded family. Nor is the new elite based upon intellect, craft, or character. Our new commercial aristocracies are built upon money.

The money need not be ours. It can be someone else's. It can be company or government reimbursement of our expenses.

Thus our new aristocracies are premised as much upon people's jobs. Beholden to jobs for something to differentiate one individual from another, job titles determine our status.

Corporation laws generally hold the interests of shareholders above those of employees and executives, obliging companies to maximise their profits. Company directors and executives cite competition with other companies as the reason they need to control the company's costs, depressing employee salaries and benefits. They pay no more than they need to pay to recruit and retain the employees they want, while working them as hard as they can without losing them, at least not all at once.

Conversely, directors and executives cite competition to increase *their* fees and salaries. Directors' fees are best determined in consultation with major investors, over glasses of cognac in a private club lounge. If they were subject to the same market forces as employee remuneration, those fees would plummet. There are no jobs easier, better paid by the hour, or for which there is less accountability than public company directorships.

Directorial self-interest finds commercial reasons for a company not to give employees something it gives directors, maintaining the lifestyle to which directors are accustomed and keeping employees to the lifestyles to which directors think employees should remain accustomed. So many things, trivial and important, we perceive in terms of people's relative status or class. Sustenance means a much better class of food and wine for the rich than it does for the rest.

Never mind the welfare state that Americans devised before World War II and Europeans expanded upon afterwards. A poor person's safety net is a few coins in a fountain aside executive safety nets.

A director's tribe, if there is one, is not normally any one company, for directors normally serve on several company boards. Their tribes, if they have any, are other directors and the most senior of executives: their post-racial sense of what they must be.

They are unlikely to enjoy any tribe. When directors feel their interests are at stake, they abandon each other as easily as they abandon anyone else, even if their self-interest keeps the directorial safety nets in place.

They join clubs without meetings, which they attend anyway. In private rooms and clubs ensconced away from the world, they dine among their own, where the people they have harmed cannot walk in upon them. If they think of those people they will never again see, then it might be to laugh. When they talk, they applaud each other's success. They blame people they will not see again for all failure.

At tables and in chairs around them are their peers, who rarely bother them. They would join another club if those peers did.

For all our comfort and envy, we are forever individuals. Without love from the commercial aristocracy for everyone else, there is no love from everyone else for the commercial aristocracy. The greatest disdain for the elite comes from people close enough to meet it: the commercial middle class.

Management

As individuals, we might be fearful and weak. With the authority of our company – our pretence of tribe and of nation – we are bold and strong.

Leaders inspire, most often by example. Managers instruct. With the power to command, there is no need to persuade, nor thought to inspire.

For managers unable to command real personal authority, job titles create and replace real self-confidence. Managers market themselves to each other and themselves.

Managers do not care if people cannot connect words into phrases, if conversations are not part of their jobs. Managers become more comfortable ordering and obeying than interacting with people.

Only the unnatural West makes economic rights synonymous with democratic rights. The right to carry on business is the right to treat employees, suppliers, and customers as we choose. We call it flexibility.

Never is a social king or queen more fixated with fashions than company executives keeping up with management fads. We need only to know something is modern business thinking to follow it.

Management theorists claim that treating employees well is good for business. Businesspeople do not really believe them, not as regards their employees. The right to free association is the right to fire someone: a right to no association.

Employees too have their rights. Being free individuals, they can leave one company in pursuit of another, but companies have become much alike. They can study, train, work more hours, or lower their expectation for income, but their only real choice is often to leave companies altogether: to be unemployed.

Western capitalism was once the freedom of people to work, earn, and spend. Without race and nation, it gave way to an individualist capitalism without so much freedom. We promote freedom with a passion, but not for each other.

Too many freedoms leave us without freedom at all: freedoms without freedom. Freedom is for people in charge.

Corporations as Fiefdoms

Western individualism is our rejection of authority over us. It is also our rejection of everything keeping us from telling others what to do.

As often as not, we are pursuing authority over others. Without tribalism, power is a company manager's alone: a means to exercise his individual interest, doing whatever she wants without regard for anyone else. It is an individual right, as are the only rights individualists comprehend. Powerful people offer no more than magnanimity to those over whom they have power.

Employees defer, at least publicly, to more senior positions. They try to find personal powers and happiness as best as they can, with no more regard for the powerful than the powerful feel for them.

To shape somebody's life, we do not need to be politically or economically all-powerful. We do not need to be more powerful than everyone else. We simply need a little more power than somebody else. We are solitary people who, in the story of our lives, often have no greater impact upon other people's lives than we find in our tiny offices.

The most that some employees ever control are our personal workspaces. Some employees do not even control that. All that some managers control are other people's workplaces.

Corporations become fiefdoms; we do not frown upon

feudalism as we frown upon nationalism. Without someone to tell us, we cannot see the trauma within other people's offices. We can, from afar, seem rather sad.

If medieval serfs had freedom to move from one fiefdom to another, there was not much reason to do so. From even the most tyrannical of lords, they could not go very far.

Nor can employees today. We nevertheless trust enough in free markets for where it will lead.

Morality and Ethics

Much morality was traditionally common across races and cultures, but our individualism denies us recognition of it. Instead, we see the variations of morality between races and cultures. The unnatural West does not want variance. Moral relativism denies that any Western morality is better than any other morality.

Amidst a myriad of races and cultures and thus a myriad of moralities, ethics provides norms to which the unnatural West wants us all to subscribe. Thus, ethics supplanted morality.

In our Age of Ideology, something is good because it complies with ideology: because human authorities declare it to be good. Ethics are humanist.

Morality is judgemental and intolerant. Ethics are conciliatory and inclusive.

Western employers and customers do not want right from wrong. Employers want obedience. Customers want service. Commercial marketplaces care no more about someone's sense of right or wrong than about his hair colour or the width of her eyebrows.

Morality can be corrupting. Christians call greed, jealousy, and selfishness immoral, but they are all ethical. They might even be mandatory.

There are few things more damaging to a person's reputation in the unnatural West than a strong sense of morality. Connoting God and Christianity, morality became a matter to mention only in church, where others cannot hear. We do well to keep morality secret.

Employers, clients, and investors might allow morality in people's personal lives, but do not allow much scope to have personal lives. People without morality at work will hardly stumble upon it in the rest of their lives.

Amorality and immorality are not confined to corporations. The same amorality and immorality we see inside Western companies we see outside them, even if it is manifest in different ways.

What remain are the mores of commerce: what is not prohibited must be allowed. Personal morality is the morality of buying. If it *feels* good, then it must *be* good.

Consumer morality comes without shame and guilt, unless we want shame and guilt. We have the right to choose what we feel. It is all ethical.

Our new norms reduce ultimately to working. The only immoralities are those affecting the sorry way we work. An executive's personal life might be completely amoral, but only becomes unethical if more senior businesspeople believe that amorality could affect the company business.

Rights and self-interest replaced righteousness and self-sacrifice. Managers and marketers replaced heroes and villains. Profit and loss replaced good and evil.

Laws and Ethics

Without nationalism or collective religion, laws and ethics are the only fetters on us pursuing our individual interests. Theoretically, laws determine what people *must* do. Ethics determine what people *should* do.

When professional associations discipline members for unethical conduct or when employers fire employees for breach, ethics become like laws. Otherwise, in practice, we are less likely to comply with ethics. They are only ethics.

Ethics are one thing. Justice and individual self-interest are others. If the unnatural West is not predicated upon justice to justify all manner of wrongdoing, then it is predicated upon individual self-interest. We equate justice with individual self-interest, when we are the individuals.

Trusting experts as we do, committees often formalise ethics. They are whatever powerful people want them to be because human authorities, not God or a tribal conscience, determine them.

Like laws, ethics are rules to impose upon others. They are

other people's ethics.

For employees, the marketplace determining our ethics is our employer. Employees have ethical duties to work as they are told to work, and to act and not act outside from work as the employer dictates. Employers suffer no duties to employees, beyond any the law imposes, and not even those duties if many employers can help it.

No ethics require a manager giving instructions to others to comply with those instructions himself. Put another way, hypocrisy is not unethical; it does us no harm. Indeed, corporate governance depends upon people without ethics affecting them still knowing enough about ethics to dictate the behaviour of others.

Ethics are more concerned with employee duties to employers than to other employees. Undermining our colleagues is perfectly ethical. We call it ambition. We have the right to malign.

Financial advisors, as much as their clients, like to talk of advisers owing ethical duties to their clients. It is good marketing, excusing the way they treat everyone else.

What might otherwise be unethical behaviour is not unethical if the people to whom the ethics are owed do not mind. Different marketplaces demand different ethics.

If our compliance with ethics does not depend upon punishment for being caught doing wrong, it requires reward. Ethics are duties we owe people who pay us or entrust money to us; they need to know we will act in their interests. The reward of ethics is the customers' confidence to buy, the employers' confidence to employ, or the investors' confidence to invest. Ethics promote economic activity.

The judgement of ethics is the consumer boycotting a business. Small investors sell shares or withhold further funding. Large investors discipline management.

The Imagery of Ethics

Ethics are rules and procedures to follow most carefully, so that other people can see they are followed most carefully. The scrutiny of ethics, like laws, shapes the formalities of carrying on business and evidence of those formalities, without changing anything substantial anyone does. They mould the way decisions are documented, leaving a satisfactory trail in company records. Neither ethics nor laws disturb business.

Directors are never more active than they are promoting the interests of other businesses in which they are concerned. Even if laws or ethics require individual directors to appear distant from decisions affecting their personal interests, directors recognise each other's interests well enough for their decisions to assist each other, as long as they personally do not suffer. Readers relying solely upon minutes of meetings presume attendees do not communicate elsewhere or are stupid.

Commercial necessity requires people to care what people with whom they conduct business think of them: the people to whom they market themselves. The imagery of ethics is the ethical person being seen by the marketplace to be ethical. It is public relations: reputation rather than honour.

Ethics are marketers' morality, driven by other people's expectations. Actions nobody else notices cannot be unethical. Many a supposedly competitive tender process is carried out purely to appoint a particular tenderer, selected before the process begins. If the marketplace wanting ethical conduct is unaware of a breach, the breach means zilch.

The marketplace determining what is ethical need only be a minority of the whole population, if the rest do not care. Their zeal empowers the few.

Still, ethics are popular or they would not be ethics. They would be laws.

People act ethically, unless doing so is to their disadvantage. The more piffling the ethical requirement, the more trivial its consequence, the easier it is to comply.

Without tribalism, we have lost our humanity. Ethics are generally not concerned with people being hurt.

Individualism affords us ethics, but ethics do not go very far. Without a marketplace wanting ethics, there are no ethics.

Ethics only apply to carrying on business. There are no ethics for consumers buying goods and services.

Nor are there ethics for the conduct of personal lives, to the extent personal lives remain. Anyone relying solely upon Western laws and ethics has little guidance to personal relationships.

The Right to Lie

Cheerfulness does not mean people are not maintaining barriers around them. The adjunct to Western individualism is the acute privacy by which we guard ourselves, except to the extent our individual self-interest warrants disclosure. Whenever reputation serves our ambition, we pass around our carefully crafted business cards. We draft our computer site profiles accordingly.

Exhibitionism is not intimacy. It can be marketing. Whatever private people reveal of themselves might be real or contrived, but is almost always controlled.

A businessperson's ethical obligations can be to lie, when other people's money is at stake. The truth matters less than the company result.

Conversely, telling the truth can be unethical. Honesty can be selfish, when other people suffer financially as a result.

Lying to employees is often legal and ethical, retaining and motivating them when the truth would unsettle them. Legal prohibitions on lying in trade and commerce do not prevent lies *within* companies.

People say whatever they feel they need to say, even if they do not really need to say it. They say whatever they want to say.

Without thought of morality but heaps of equality, we do not discriminate against the dishonest. People's lies are less often a Machiavellian conviction that ends justify their means than a complete indifference between fact and falsehood. Indifference between truthfulness and deceit is indifference to other people.

We have not much of a right to tell the truth, but we have quite the right to lie. Bluffing is dishonesty that other people accept, knowing they too will bluff when they can. Honest people do not bluff, but honesty can harm negotiations as much in business as in buying a house, car, or anything else.

Lies can be clever. Telling the truth can be lazy.

Knowledge has become no less transient than everything else in our unnatural West. What matters is the conviction with which people impart it.

The more dishonest the words, the more often and more forcefully people need to repeat them. Lies are more difficult to recall than are facts, but some lies are repeated often enough for even the liars to forget they were lies.

The Right to Suppress the Truth

A right to lie is not much of a right if people cease trusting a person because they learn that he or she lies. Self-interest deters most people from lying to someone who will eventually learn they were lying.

People lying freely to others can get upset about others lying to them, when those lies cost them time or money. Unless being the bearer of bad news is a problem or we are not meant to know something, telling people what they are going to find out anyway is normally prudent, but they might never find out.

Societies were predicated upon people having some idea what they were doing, but individuals are not societies. Among our endless rights, we have the right to be stupid. We are free to be foolish.

We have the right to be wrong. An untruth is only a lie if the person uttering it knows it to be untrue, or has a reckless disregard whether it is true or untrue.

A person's right to stupidity is not much of a right if other people see he is stupid. To give effect to a right to be stupid, horrible, or anything else unpopular without suffering for being seen to be so, requires the right to suppress the truth.

The more damaging the facts, the more important is the right to conceal them. Our right to suppress the truth can become an ethical obligation to more senior company officers and our employers, investors, or suppliers to do so.

In our freedom to choose, we do not choose shame. We cast whatever more commercial and other damage we need to cast if that conceals past lies and errors, in the exercise of our right to look good.

The Right to Ignorance

Our traditional British and other Western social etiquette has become another fetter on us individuals doing whatever we want to do. The hindrances irritating us can be the most minor of rules by which a society, including a commercial society, function.

Without social etiquette, we have lost business etiquette. Individualism means the end of etiquette.

Merely being misled by a liar is not a loss. The lies that rile us are lies costing us money or time.

In a West that no longer values the facts, lies that do not cost us money or time are not victimless wrongs. They are not wrongs at all. There is no end of victimless lies.

Conversely, the truth can cost more than a lie. The best truths are free.

Managers do not like employees too honest. They are terrified of what they might say. The new corporate etiquette demands employees not tell their managers anything needlessly inconvenient or unsettling, such as something in which those managers ethically should involve themselves when they would much rather not.

Whenever company officers and managers are culpable for employees' illegal activities, they set up systems of corporate governance and monitoring not to prevent employees acting illegally, but to be their defence to being prosecuted when employees do act illegally. If those officers and managers are making money from those activities benefiting the company results, their individual interests make them prefer not to know those systems have failed. To avoid unwanted advice, they ensure that people who might have something unwelcome to reveal report to others. The only people more troublesome than current employees are past ones.

We have a right to ignorance: the innocence of ignorance. The only thing worse to hear than a lie is the truth.

Consumption

Other races do not reduce their lives to commercial transactions as we do. They have their families, races, and thus their cultures.

The less we in the unnatural West enjoy our families and races, the more we think we need material things. It is all very well to complain about consumerism, but without races or other tribes bigger than ourselves, we are without religion and other culture. We need something in which to believe.

What remains is whatever free markets afford us: shopping and work. We store our credence in whatever we do, buy, and eat. We are workers and consumers: our minds set for toiling, dining, and drinking.

Food and wine are something to discuss other than work, without revealing personal matters in a restaurant any more than inside an office. Discussing other people's consumption, we reveal even less.

Consumption makes all the trial and tedium of work worthwhile, alleviating the pointlessness, boredom, and stress from the rest of our lives. When someone walks into a store with the air of being willing to buy, even the lowliest of employees is suddenly in control of his life. For that fleetingly brief time before a vendor trying to make him a sale, he is empowered. The vendor is courteous, smiling even, whatever she really is thinking. She might flirt and fawn, until he looks away.

The power of purchase is the only power most of us experience. Purchasing power seems very masculine, haggling over the price to pay in a game to be won. Spending is also our feminine side: fashion and flair.

Our rampant capitalism becomes rampant materialism; most of us have nothing else. Our devotion to the products we purchase can be fierce.

With our consumption, we are again tribal, united by a brand name. Product imagery has become more prolific in the unnatural West than imagery from our waning people pasts: flags, crests, and seals. We might cringe at the sight of a national flag, but never at the sight of a corporate logo. The tribes we form by the things that we buy become the tribes we no longer need mention, but we know they are there.

We care about brands. Customers pay more money for the same products because they come with a brand. The price of admission to the tribe is a price we are willing to pay, so we like paying a bit more for the symbol we proudly display. It is the people we become by our purchase.

When we buy, we are again human beings, up to a commercially relevant point. Hidden from view, whenever the realities of people who purchase their products demand it, marketers acknowledge those facets of people the unnatural West otherwise ignores: race, religion, and so forth.

With race, there are nations to hold. Vendors wave any flag or tout any national logo they think customers favour.

With race, there is a cultural heritage upon which vendors can draw. We have religious heritages, if not religion.

With religion too, customers have creeds and morality. Advertisers might mould them but not wilfully offend them.

When we are consumers, we are again men or women. Men are again fathers, married men without children, or bachelors. Women are again mothers, married without children, or spinsters. (When spinsters sounded old, they became bachelorettes.) Once our demographic details become clear, we are not so individual at all.

Those traits matter more than our work and our wealth, provided we have money to spend. We buy back part of the lives we lost in our ideals and other people's ideologies. Something to buy or we have bought means we slip quietly away, just for a time, from being mere individuals. It all depends on the product, geography, and time.

Greed

If marketing makes everything seem perfect, then the trouble with living in a supposedly perfect place is that there is nothing left for us to do, were it not for our greed. Without nationalism or God to inspire us, we have greed.

Pursuing money or anything else with a determined and dogged desire, even to excess, is not greed when it is pursued at nobody's expense. Greed is pursuing anything to excess at other people's expense, unfairly denying other people something they need when we do not need any more. Thus greed was immoral when we were races and nations, because we cared about those people that our greed would deny.

Greed is no longer immoral in the unnatural West because we are individuals. We are no longer concerned with those other people.

No amount of anything can be enough. Behind greed in production of all the more goods and services lies greed in consumption, but not necessarily for the same goods and services. We will do anything for money.

There is no tribal greed without tribes. Behind corporate greed is personal greed by people who benefit by the corporate greed, even if only to their reputation or ego. We are too much the individuals for the greed motivating us to be anything but personal. Without a personal interest at stake, we are quite ambivalent about company money.

With our disinterest in *saving* company money is our great joy *spending* company money: the power and happiness that comes from expenditure without cost. Food never tastes so flavoursome, wine never so supple, as when the company pays. There can be no more efficient purchase by our employer than one providing us with the joys of consumption in the sureties of our strident careers.

Spending company money on ourselves is self-interest, which is always ethical. That is, provided the people to whom we owe ethics do not notice.

Company interests matter when individual interests are not in play. When time comes to spend company money upon others, our ethics expect us to act frugally, as if the money were ours.

No function is more closely identified with managerial seniority than reviewing other people's expense claims. Some managers take pleasure doing so. It might be all that they do.

Greed became the single-word adjective to describe Western capitalism (thus Western individualism), although away from financial markets, businesspeople prefer words like hunger, drive, and ambition. To dwell upon greed is to ignore everything else happening.

Careers

When our vocations became matters of focus centuries ago, with goals and directions, there came the idea of careers. They were public service careers instead of staying forever a clerk. Military careers meant rising through officer ranks, rather than remaining a foot soldier.

We called lawyers, doctors, nurses, and teachers professional people because professions were not ignoble jobs, let alone careers with their obvious hierarchies. In our times of races and nations, professions answered a popular good without thought of reward. Lawyers and doctors could afford to be noble, being normally well rewarded.

When we lost our senses of nation, we lost our senses of national good. Our only interests became our individual own. Professions became careers. Professional careers became more careers than professions.

Without tribes there is no common purpose, not even for the most mundane of matters. There is only individual purpose.

With no one else to consider, individuals work for themselves, if we work at all. Our careers are for our personal gain, not anyone else's. All that matters is what our work does for us; the only outcomes that count are ours.

As well as funding the rest of our lives, our careers are pursuits for their own sakes: ends to themselves, with powers and feelings for which we still yearn. If we work to succeed then our success lies in our senses of work. Careers are for people who want more to their lives than consuming goods and services all of the time.

Without a people whose achievements we share, our only successes are those individually ours. Other people's work does not matter, unless we find ourselves a role in it.

To find our success when all we have is our individual selves, we need not look very far. We need not look beyond the end of our chairs.

Marketing everything sold means we market ourselves, without admitting it. Self-promotion should be subtle, but there can be no humility.

Without tribalism to inspire us to something greater than ourselves, we need merely to appear to work well. What matters is what people think we do, not what we actually do. We need only convince others we give them what they require. Marketing becomes merit, as much for people as products.

Busyness

Political economics connects political and social considerations to the study of economics. Late in the eighteenth century, Scottish political economist Adam Smith's many insights included observing that the purpose of economic production is its ultimate consumption.

Since then, we have become too preoccupied with our individual interests to care about the consequences of our work upon others. Our work is the means to *our* consumption, not anyone else's, so we do not need to produce anything, provided we earn money. Producing something might get in our way.

Proving our usefulness to others does not require us to be

useful. It requires us to appear to be useful, however inconsequential we are.

Businesspeople saying we are busy mean our businesses are successful, although we are never too busy to welcome that special new customer. Employees of other people's businesses saying we are busy mean we are personally successful, but too busy to take on anything more.

Employees do not need to be busy. We need to be seen to be busy.

In jobs without work, having no work to perform is no reason for people not to barrel around offices as if pursuing all-important missions. Employees create a meek aura of work high around them, demonstrating their usefulness even if only by repeating each other's work.

Employees saying (not complaining) we are busy affirm that our employers are paramount in our lives. Leaving our workplaces at the end of a day says we are not, unless we explain we are headed to work elsewhere.

Instead of working, we manage. Managers demonstrate their usefulness by growing the numbers of people reporting to them however little any of them do, or by reducing those numbers of people reporting to them however much those people did.

We are in busyness more than business, not necessarily busyness working. Perpetual motion belies the pointlessness of it all.

Sometimes actors realise they are putting on a show. They manipulate their audience, which has come to be manipulated. Sometimes they are accidental actors, the audience no less accidental.

Marketers have become hustlers. Companies do not take our last semblance of souls by working us so hard or so little, but by us lying so much about it. Pretending to be like the hustlers around us, means we are like the hustlers around us. Lying often enough about the people we are, can turn lies into the truth.

Work as Occupation

Time at a workplace has ceased to be time to complete useful tasks. It is a predetermined period needing to be filled.

Work is occupation: whatever occupies time. We equate time with performance. Efficiency becomes laziness, if it means spending less time at a task.

Sometime beyond merely being in our workplaces, we became comfortable there. We do not want efficiency to mean we perform less work or the same work in less time. We are not thinking of more money, although we take all the money we can. We might have already earned more than we will spend. We just want something to do, however little the result. Occupation became a reward in itself, important for its own sake, without function or consequence. Our lives became time evading time.

With the only roles left to us those in our jobs, we can want a lot more. We can want all the things we wanted when we had nations and religion, although we want them as free individuals. We want them for ourselves.

Without communities, we have come to expect our careers to be our social networks too. When our only identity is the work that we do, we want validation.

Some people need something more, for the small station it gives them among people who do not like them at all. The most important social welfare function of our individualist West is to give insignificant small people, who would otherwise be cowering in corners pulling the wings from houseflies, the chance to feel important.

They do not have to be important. They need only feel important.

Mortal Corporations

The companies that replaced Western countries no longer amount to much. Sometime after our national interests gave way to sectional interests, those sectional interests also gave way.

Corporations have come to mean little, but there is still economics. Western corporations, like Western countries, have become the means of individuals exercising their economic and other individual interests. That might mean carrying on business, or might mean shutting the business down. We call it free enterprise.

The more individualistic we have become, the smaller our lives have become. Corporations need only serve individual interests a short time. When they no longer serve some individuals, the individuals depart. When they no longer serve the people in charge, the corporations depart. It is the same with Western countries.

Amidst our transient individualism, corporations last less time than careers. Relationships are for company tenure, at most, not for life.

Companies are never more facile and careers never more futile than when we are not just readying to leave, but are picking apart the carcass of a company preparing to close down. What once seemed important proved in time to be all just reams of thick paper and billions of electronic bits. Our best work was always our work for ourselves, our personal pursuits. Ours have again become jobs without career.

Jobs can be fun, informative, and intellectually engaging, but so are plenty of other activities. Without races, religions, or any other greater purpose than our individual selves, what matters about a job is money.

Capitalism with a Human Face

As long ago as the seventeenth century, French nobleman François de La Rochefoucauld spoke of individual self-interest and self-love being important motivations, without excluding other considerations. Without nations or other tribes, we have lost those other considerations.

Traditional nineteenth-century anarchy was not a rejection of society. It was a rejection of government.

Without nationalism or other tribalism to replace the structures of government, anarchy becomes chaos and conflict. The anarchy of individualism gives way to despotic dictatorship by the most powerful.

Our governments, corporations, and other bodies are as immoral as the people who run them, but describing profit-maximising corporations in the unnatural West as psychopaths became trite. In truth, we are no more or less psychopathic than the corporations we occupy. If it is hard to believe the long-desk psychopaths in white shirts or black skirts running large companies, then we need only see the psychopaths who are not running them. Businesspeople are no more or less psychopathic than is anyone else in the unnatural West.

However little we acknowledge it, we lack the senses of tribe, empathy, and morality to treat each other fairly without laws compelling us to do so. Without nationalism or Christianity, we need more regulation than we needed with them. Without social mores or morality to move us, we need laws to restrict us.

What human laws do not forbid, they allow. Our Western predisposition is to be free to do whatever we want to do, unless there is good reason otherwise. Sometimes, there is good reason.

A world of rights without obligations is no place to carry on business. To trade, people need to rely upon others.

Preoccupied with our commercial liberties, we often disregard the benefits to us of laws regulating others. Others disregard the benefit of regulating us, but we know how decent we are.

Liberalising people's lives in liberal free market democracies means imposing controls on human activity. Individualism necessitates laws to protect employers and employees, vendors and buyers, and everyone else.

Uniform regulations wisely developed fetter us from doing whatever we want to do. More importantly, they protect us from others doing whatever they want to do. We know the perils that other people's liberties can be.

We thus correct some of the failings of unbridled individualism, without denying economic realities. We need laws to require other people not to mislead us and to honour their commitments to us, although only in trade and commerce.

Only governments can foist greater public interests upon individuals unwilling to sense any good beyond our individual interests, although governments just as easily foist narrow sectional interests if not much greater evils. Government is the body best able to protect and the body best able to oppress.

Without a people to keep us, government's role is to massage the markets: capitalism with a human face. We regulate individuals' behaviour in business much as we regulate it elsewhere, moderating jungle economics and relentless capitalism along our way towards civil economics and managed capitalism. The optimum degree of regulation (much like the optimum degree of everything else) varies according to the people, place, and time. The challenge for governments is to manage capitalism without managing companies: regulating human activity without controlling human beings.

Labour Laws

Our courts decided that companies have the minds of key directors and managers. Much harder than ascribing companies with minds is ascribing them with hearts.

Labour is intrinsically the most imperfect of markets. Coming from the free market side and before reaching the optimum, the more labour is regulated, the less imperfect a market it is.

From an employer's point of view, laws made in calm analysis save us from committing the worst of our tyranny of individualism. From an employee's point of view, they can save us from the tyranny of other people's individualism. Many a manager is effectively both employer and employee.

Without nationalism connecting them in their common interests, employee excesses can be no less harmful than employer excesses. They can deter businesses from employing the unemployed or drive businesses into oblivion.

Laws defend not only the weak but the strong: millionaires directing big companies as much as paupers sweeping the streets. They protect righteous heroes from wrongdoing villains: the magnanimous from the mean.

Governments cannot legislate for compassion, but compassionate employers need laws to force upon their cruel competitors what compassionate employers do anyway. Humanity rarely makes good business sense.

Competition prejudices businesses generously rewarding their employees or trimming their work hours by increasing their costs relative to their competitors. Callous employers unscrupulously minimising employees' salaries or working employees harder can thus charge customers less for their products and services. Consumers indifferent to Western employees (although often concerned greatly about workers of other races) would rather pay less for the same, so the businesses more generous to their employees are more likely to fail.

Without nationalism and its consequential morality, nothing less than enforced legislation ensure employees' minimum wages, maximum working hours, holidays, notice periods for dismissal, and parental, carers', and sick leave. Redundancy payments need only be formulaic estimates of employee salaries until they find equivalent jobs, without moving their homes and unduly disrupting their families. They afford vulnerable employees a little of the security that executives would rather keep for themselves.

Denying businesses the chance to unfairly shed or otherwise disadvantage employees means they must explore other measures to minimise their costs. It pressures them to improve their processes.

There should be nothing wrong if they cannot improve those processes anymore. Process improvement cannot be infinite.

If costs remain equal because employee and other costs remain equal, then prices equalise. That promotes competition between products and services about something other than price. It turns consumers' minds back to quality.

Law Enforcement

The Holocaust had been legal under Nazi German law. Thus after the war, being lawful slowly ceased being a reason to do something.

Resistance to the Nazi regime had been illegal. Thus after the war, being unlawful slowly ceased being a reason not to do something.

In an ideal society of people ideal, there might be no call for police. Otherwise, police have proven no less necessary in business than they are on the streets in the individualist, multiculturalist West. At least on the streets, the victim has some kind of a chance.

Allowing individuals self-regulation is at best no regulation. At worst, it is like putting a leopard in charge of a deer park.

Individuals are the narrowest of narrow libertarians. We want to regulate other people's behaviour without losing our rights to do whatever we want to do.

If laws forbid what we want to do, we might deem the laws wrong. We might blame them upon other people's political or economic objectives we reject. Conversely, we might like a law insofar as it controls other people and thereby protects us, but exercise our right to breach it, if we can get away with it.

The right to break a law we dislike becomes another human right, amidst our endlessly expanding bevy of rights. We might sanctimoniously call our lawbreaking civil disobedience, as if we were civil and there was something heroic about us, much like our view of the resistance to Nazism, but we are simply doing whatever self-serving individuals want to do.

That is no less true of people outside business than inside it. Laws mean little if they are not enforced.

Senior businesspeople normally know their companies' legal obligations. If the police, securities commissions, and other government agencies by whatever name are not enforcing parliament's laws then management will not.

An audit committee chairman's primary competence is not ensuring a company complies with its legal obligations, as business theory presumes and laws demand. It is ensuring that no corporate catastrophe costs him money or soils her reputation.

At best, businesspeople assess the costs of their companies complying with the law and whether illegal actions are worth the risks and consequences to the company of being caught in a breach and prosecuted. If lawyers cannot finds means of achieving the ends that managers want without breaking the law (for a reasonable cost), then businesspeople expect lawyers to find means by which the company is least likely to be caught. Legal compliance is a rational commercial decision.

At worst, like other individuals, businesspeople do not care whether their companies comply with the law. Other people might, for which we have courts, plaintiffs, and litigation, but complaints, court action, and insurance premia are no reason to deter executives and employees from scrounging more money than they cost the company and themselves by the way they carry on business.

Legal obligations upon companies need not perturb directors, managers, or employees, unless it is in their interest they do. The company's interest is not theirs, unless the law or company makes it so.

Companies are most likely to honour laws if directors and managers are personally liable for breaches, bringing their executive interest into play. Any penalties that individual directors and managers incur matter far more to them than any penalties incurred by the companies they direct and manage.

Trade practices (anti-trust) laws are laws for the sake of economies, not necessarily people. Health and safety laws might be too, for advocates arguing that illness, injuries, and death matter for their economic effects.

Without regulation, many a manager would be a killer. With

regulation, he is merely a tyrant, as far as the law making him personally culpable allows.

Laws are poor substitutes for tribalism and thus morality. Companies may well honour the strict letter of their legal obligations, but no more.

Western Socialism

People only comprise a society when they think and act collectively. When we throw the onus of helping people onto society without the nationalism or other tribalism by which we are among the people willing to help, we are absolving ourselves of responsibility. Without tribalism, we are calling upon a society that no longer exists.

Consuming politics much as customers consume everything else, never finding contentment, Western socialism has become a long string of gripes and grievances about what governments and corporations ought to do, rather than what socialists themselves do. There is no greater individualist than the socialist imploring society to do something, while finding excuses personally not to do that something. Western socialism becomes another ideology of individualism.

As obsessed with commerce as anyone else without thought of race, nation, and culture, there are few problems for which Western socialists think the cure is not money, primarily payments for welfare. Employee and consumer protection they frame within monetary ideals, declaring them good for business or the economy, without thought of morality.

Self-interest can make people generous, with other people's money. The wealth that socialists want to redistribute is not their wealth but other people's wealth; some people are very altruistic with other people's interests. Rich people are people richer than they are: socialism for a socialist aristocracy.

Class warfare might drive it; most lives involve some form of conflict. If there is a class on whose behalf an individual fights, with him at the centre, it is a very small class.

Western socialism might be no more than a need to be liked. Self-serving generosity is generosity nevertheless; among the collateral damage our individualism wreaks is some collateral good.

Socialist badges pressed into capitalist hearts mean a few drops of chilled blood fall down to the floor.

Facts

We were not born this way. We became this way.

Without morality, we have no desire for truth because we have no concern for the consequences of lies and falsehoods upon others. We need and have rights to so much in our unnatural West, but have no rights to the facts.

Without facts, what have we? We have nothing. At the heart and through the breadth of our ideological West is make-believe so compelling we ground our politically constructed reality in it, but it is make-believe nevertheless.

Instead of deferring to human authorities, we could pursue truth ourselves, including truth about people and God. We could value the truth more than transactions, facts more than fallacies. We could prefer facts to ideals, including those about human biology, nature, and culture. Instead of deciding what we would like reality to be, we could consider what reality is: a pursuit instead of a decision.

Consensus should be no more than a convenient commencement point in our pursuit of the facts. Consensus changes over time. Consensus differs between races and places. Majority opinions in the West are not those across the rest of the world, not anymore. They might never have been.

A myriad of facts come to light when we pause from our presumptions. A million people marching to slogans or clicking their approval on a computer site mean less than one person with a pertinent fact or logical argument. Debates do not end by being avoided.

Preferring reality to unreality is a choice, but facts are more freeing than people imagine. For the most part, facts are consistent and predictable. They are simple, straightforward, and easy, even if pursuing knowledge about them is not.

Feelings change. Ideas pass. Lies dissolve.

We could seek something real in which to believe. At the end of the day and at the beginning, we want either to know facts or to lose truth in ideology, about anything. No person, family, or race can survive without dealing with reality.

Self-Awareness

For all our useless self-absorption, we lack useful self-awareness, never as good at seeing faults in ourselves as we see faults in others. We cannot see our craziness. We cannot see our self-destruction.

There is no greater burden upon people than espousing loyalty to those who scold us for our loyalty, but our people are no less our people for being disloyal. The unnatural West's problems come not from capitalism, but from individualism. Without natural tribal identities, the only returns we imagine are to individuals.

Self-serving individuals expect other individuals to be just as self-serving as they are. We expect others to do as they please.

No matter how kind other people's actions might be, we interpret them with the assumption those people act from individual self-interests: the only interests we individualists comprehend. The unnatural West no longer thinks in terms of tribe or morality, so cannot comprehend people who do.

Some people said communism collapsed because people could never be selfless, that human beings remained sufficiently selfish to demand return for their labour, but people can be selfless when they share a common identity. With a collective identity come nationalism and other tribalism. Their tribe is also their self.

The more individualistic we are, the nastier we are. We are horrible most of all to each other.

We might talk of being progressive and progressive politics, but there is nothing progressive about abandoning human nature or our family, race, and civilisation. It is regressive.

The universe does not change because we long for it to change. Human nature does not change because we ignore it, try to manage it, or try to change it.

A century after we began dispensing with race and Christianity, the unnatural West has failed to come up with anything better to shape our relations with each other. When we ceased caring about our countries, we ceased caring about each other. When we ceased answering to God and our ancestors, we answered to no one.

The unnatural West might have been able to afford abandoning

God or our nations, but not both. We can afford to discard almost everything, but human nature.

An End to Ideology

Resisting ideologies can feel like trying to hold back the tide, but tides are natural. Tides also go back.

Communist lies said there was only oppression and poverty among the capitalist democracies, but when East Europeans glimpsed over the stark Berlin Wall or through gaps in the cruel Iron Curtain, they saw material prosperity. They stopped believing the communists.

In 1989, the Berlin Wall fell. In 1991, the Soviet Union disintegrated.

Certain that human history had ended with the advent of their supposedly perfect society, communism had previously seemed interminable. It collapsed, for having been so far from perfect after all.

Since then, the West has reflected the same arrogance with individualism. Individualism could fall too, evolve into something better, or devolve into something worse.

Individualism could evolve or devolve without change to our corporate individualist capitalism or, more likely, with economic changes as well. That something better or worse might then make way for something else anew or something old again. We could change some way back to being the people we once were, without losing the good things we enjoy and most likely enjoying more.

If our new Western ways wane, then they might well wane from within. We will look deep inside ourselves, and see something basic sorely neglected. We will consider other races, and see the natures in them we have lost sight of in ourselves: the nationalism, racism, and other tribalism; any empathy they feel or morality they practice. We will confront the reality of the world around us and question what we are doing and what we have been told.

In such event, ideologies will be found wanting. We will thus yearn, individually and collectively, to take back our lives from human authorities.

Facts and ideas matter because people matter. They matter quite apart from the human authority or lack of authority that a person who utters a fact or idea holds.

The West would not be going backwards if we resume a path that most of the world never left. We would be going forwards again, as we were until the Great War. This Age of Ideology will end.

An Age of Re-Enlightenment

An Age of Re-Enlightenment might start. The West will return to reason.

We will return to acting naturally as other races continue to do, allowing ourselves to think and feel naturally: tribally. Our unadulterated human instincts are objective standards, however subjective might be our efforts to express them.

More than self-interest, we could choose self-realisation, bringing up our attributes from within. We need to make time and space to be human, based in biology, and feel what it inspires.

We could be what human beings are, with our glorious failings and inglorious strengths. We could bask in being men and women, biologically brilliant and flawed, trying to get a little bit better. Without the arrogance to think there is freedom in trying to change human nature, we could find freedom by fulfilling our natures.

We might feel as our forebears felt, becoming what we can be: peoples enjoying being ourselves. We will sense something greater than our momentary commercial interests: a greater well-being than anything economic.

We presume the only hunger is for money and material things, but we could find again hunger for life, love, and truth. We could find again morality, empathy, and care.

Being Western, we will cherish personal expression and liberty, not just for ourselves but also for the rest of our race. We might even facilitate them for other races, provided people of our race do not suffer as a result.

We will want again to be races and nations enjoying honour and moral decency in our dealings with each other, knowing those others will enjoy honour and moral decency in their dealings with us. We will want people who will freely help us when we need it, knowing we will freely help them when they need it.

If we are to be more than politics and economics permit us to be, then we need to be more to begin with. We need to be races and nations.

We need to learn of our peoples to learn who we are, but we cannot dwell upon what might have been but for the Great War. We must focus our minds upon what is and what will be, with what we know about what has been.

If there is a right worth having, then it is a right to a fulfilling, comfortable life. Lives are not just more valid, profound, and intrinsically more satisfying when founded upon nature rather than living in lieu of it. They are sustainable.

Wanting whatever maintains and advances our qualities of life means keeping our dreams distinct from our decisions. We could remain rabid idealists for what people can possibly be, and intelligent pragmatists for what people really are: pragmatic idealism.

Survival depends upon us being what we are, rather than trying to be what we are not. If we cannot be ourselves then nobody can, and we cannot meaningfully be anyone else.

2. THE END OF NATURAL SELECTION

At odds with what most people at the time thought to be true, Englishman Charles Darwin presented his theories of natural selection in his 1859 book *On the Origin of Species*. "*As many more individuals of each species are born than can possibly survive,*" he wrote in the book's introduction, "*and as, consequently, there is a frequently recurring struggle for existence, it follows that any being, if it vary however slightly in any manner profitable to itself, under the complex and sometimes varying conditions of life, will have a better chance of surviving, and thus be naturally selected. From the strong principle of inheritance, any selected variety will tend to propagate its new and modified form.*"

Over generations, species evolve. Through our Age of Enlightenment, we of the then natural West believed that human beings were getting better the longer the human race continued.

In *Principles of Biology*, published in 1864, British philosopher Herbert Spencer linked his economic theories with Darwin's biological theories. "*This survival of the fittest...is that which Mr. Darwin has called 'natural selection', or the preservation of favoured races in the struggle for life.*"

In *The Variation of Animals and Plants under Domestication* published in 1868, Darwin adopted Spencer's phrase. "*The term "natural selection" is in some respects a bad one, as it seems to imply conscious choice….*"

Natural selection is not necessarily a matter of being physically or mentally superior. It is a matter of fitting in best with the immediate environment. Living in the open air, a person does well to be tall. Living in caves, a person does well to be short.

All men are not created equal. Neither are all women.

Early in the twenty-first century, there is no natural selection so far as human beings are concerned. The air is neither hot nor cold inside centrally conditioned buildings. Amidst the rampant abundance of amenities and technologies, the scrawny no longer fall sick and die. They collect their medicines over the counter. The stupid take, or miss, extra classes.

The West has done something more, because the West is no longer natural. It is ideological: a peculiar political and economic environment. Few conditions of life have been more complex or varied.

Darwin was a racist and speciesist, interpreting the past and future as contests for survival between races and species. The complete title of his 1859 book was *On the Origin of Species by Means of Natural Selection, or the Preservation of Favoured Races in the Struggle for Life*.

Since the Holocaust, we have rejected contests between races. We are becoming increasingly uneasy with contests between species.

Equality

Natural selection is premised upon inclusion of some and exclusion of others, but the unnatural West insists upon inclusion of all. Everyone fits in, supposedly.

Including some and excluding others, natural selection is premised upon differences. The unnatural West is premised upon equality.

In 1776, when the West was natural, America was founded upon words and ideas drawn from European schools of philosophical thought. Thomas Jefferson's statement in the American Declaration of Independence that all men are created equal was one of fairness, not science. Americans were declaring themselves equals of the British, but also granting all Europeans in America equal opportunity in a land supposed to be without aristocracy and class.

Physical and psychological differences remained. Jefferson never doubted the reality of race, gender, and other biological differences between people. Nobody then did.

All Jefferson's Declaration of Independence really declared was a white American nationalism, in which all Europeans, essentially northern Europeans, were politically equal: especially the politically dominant British and the numerically dominant Germans. America's War of Independence replaced a distant English aristocracy with a local English aristocracy. It contemplated replacing an English king with a Prussian king, but the Prussian

Prince Henry declined.

The trouble with founding countries upon words and ideas is that words change their meanings. The way we thought changed after the Holocaust.

Our postmodern notion that all people are equal and ought to be equal owes much to Karl Marx and communism. The ideology of equality dismisses the physical and psychological differences between people (or at least any significance for those differences) as merely political constructions accorded significance by rich and powerful people in order to divide and oppress the poor and powerless.

In the unnatural West, Marxism became mainstream, at least in that respect, imposed ironically by powerful people. Understanding Marxism requires recognition that Marxists and other ideologues often practice the very wrongs they accuse others of practicing, perhaps because they are immersed in accusing.

Ideologues replaced those imagined political constructions about the importance of physical and psychological differences between people with actual political constructions about their unimportance. They invented uniformity: a sociology of sameness. We think those physical and psychological differences between people disappear if we stop noticing them.

Embracing everyone, we insist upon everyone being equal. To that end, we insist everyone is the same. When we are not trying to make everyone the same, we are insisting they already are, not simply at some mystical level but at physical and psychological levels.

Compelled to act without fear or favour, we mandate equality. On top of that, we impose equality all over the place. Anything else, we call discrimination.

Discrimination

For centuries, discrimination was a virtue. Discrimination flowed naturally from knowledge, reason, and loyalty. Not being discriminatory was stupid, desperate, or whorish. Discrimination might have implied judgement about the matter in which discrimination occurred, before judgement became a vice in the West.

Anti-discrimination is anti-intellectualism: a refusal to consider the possibilities that particular differences might be important. When anti-discrimination denies us the chances to support our own, it is demanding disloyalty.

Some categories of discrimination became illegal to ensure they became socially unacceptable. Others simply became socially unacceptable.

"That's discrimination!" has become a short, emphatic argument against many an action or point of view. The discrimination does not need to be explained or need a descriptive adjective. It is just discrimination.

Not only does the objector assume that discrimination is reason alone not to think or do something. So does the other person, at least when the other person is white. The most the other person might say is, "No, it's not discrimination!"

Introduced in the decades following the Holocaust, Western laws prohibit certain defined discriminations in certain situations, most notably racial, religious, and gender discrimination in employment and housing. Those discriminations and situations have become more numerous through the years.

Wherever discrimination remains legal in the West, it is often unethical. We discriminate against the discriminatory.

Discrimination on the basis of height, strength, or other physical attributes became unethical, and sometimes illegal, because of their correlations with race and gender. Even police and military forces relaxed their requirements, preferring racial and gender equality over safety, law enforcement, and national defence.

We are not superficial in our physical evaluations of people. We are not evaluating people at all.

What used to be called handicaps came to be called disabilities, because they are not supposed to handicap people. Disabilities disappeared, except in dedicated parking spaces and seats on buses and trains, unless they inescapably affect a job's inherent requirements. We can be able-bodied or not, blind or able to see, without differences being of anyone's concern.

Disabilities have become characteristics. Characteristics do not matter. There are no congenital deformities, because there are no deformities.

They are a fact without judgement, so the notion of treating them became disrespectful, although they might mean a person has special needs. No longer is being average an insult and being special a compliment.

We might strive to improve economic work and commercial product, but not the people producing them. That would reek of natural selection.

Finding new extents of individualism since the unnatural West dispensed with race, we have gone onto dispense with discrimination after discrimination. Soon enough, we removed from our thinking the physical features fundamental to natural selection.

We can be of any physical form we want, especially in matters of vanity. Not merely curing us when we want to be cured, patients want cosmetic doctors to tailor our faces with lies and bodies with worse, while our ideologies of equality insist there is no reason to do so.

Natural selection has not ended altogether. Short men and ugly people remain less likely to succeed in their careers than tall men and beautiful people.

Whenever natural selection pops up, the unnatural West tries to eradicate it. Equating ugliness to race and disability, discrimination against ugly people became lookism.

Central to our ideologies of equality is our individualism. Prohibiting discrimination constrains people's opportunities to choose those with whom they are most comfortable, institutionalising the separations between them.

We deal with people during economic transactions, and need not see them again. Investors need not befriend employees, customers, or suppliers. Company managers need not revisit the people they fired.

We have commercial relationships, not personal relationships. We do not need to meet; we have agents for that. We place immediate economic considerations above everything else, maximising the range of potential workers, consumers, and suppliers. Employers want everyone at work.

The End of Excellence

Too often we say the West has replaced aristocracy with meritocracy. We have done no such thing.

Selection of people on merit would hinder our drive to diversity. Judging people by the quality of their work, product, or service, would be discriminatory.

We are not people of excellence. In the contest between excellence and diversity, we want diversity.

When we draw upon all the people of the world to further our economic, ideological, and other individual self-interests, we call it diversity. The most prolific exception to our proud ignorance about people's physical characteristics is when we laud differences between them: heterogeneity.

Our rhetoric of sameness contradicts our edicts of diversity. Diversity is difference.

Merit is never further from our thoughts than in our desire to benefit minorities. Equality demands it.

Excellence would be exclusionary. We are inclusive, no matter how stupid or inept people are.

Nobody fails. We do not want to harm children's or teachers' self-confidence by failing children at school. We do not want anything to suggest children are not equal. We prefer equality to quality.

From our schools come our adults. Universities and other educational authorities operate as businesses. They want students to pass, so they re-enrol next year.

Educational authorities not operating as businesses also want students to pass. Thus the students move along, eventually graduate, and do not re-enrol the next year.

University degrees and professional accreditations are matters of marketing, evidencing expertise that might or might not be there. Professionalism is marketed professionalism. When we do not know whether people are telling us barmy old drivel, we trust their qualifications.

Still, educational qualifications and skills mean little to company success. Some managers simply do not appoint anyone cleverer than they are. That can leave very few applicants to consider. It will almost always exclude the cleverest.

The supposed rewards of our long education prove elusive. Profitless philosophers are sent home to think about gardening, while moneymaking automatons rise through company ranks.

Some people can be very successful without unnecessary intellect holding them back. If they suffer such intellect, they best be smart enough not to reveal it.

Few employees are dismissed for incompetence. They are dismissed for insubordination.

In examining companies, all most investment analysts seem to do is trust or distrust directors. While revelations of fraud have derailed many business careers, incompetence rarely seems to affect them.

People do not become equal because we now think they are. We achieve equality as we always do: by reducing the good until everyone is as bad as the worst. Whenever all things become equal, they become the least. Equality requires mediocrity.

We prefer people to be equally stupid than suffer the ignominy of anyone being cleverer than anyone else. People are becoming dumber.

As much deliberately as by our indifference, we are driving the human species down, but human devolution does not bother the unnatural West. We are not so judgemental.

Unnatural Selection

Strong men are more likely to support economic self-reliance. Weak men are more likely to support the welfare state and economic redistribution.

In the unnatural West, the weak prevail, but we are not redistributing wealth to the physically weak but intellectually strong. That would discriminate against the intellectually weak. We are simply redistributing it.

With their natural tribal instincts intact, most races prefer *their* people prosper and procreate, linking prosperity with procreation. White people are not among them, not anymore. That would be racist.

Indifferent to human evolution as much as to our race, we are more likely to favour other races than our own, provided we personally prosper. What I call unnatural selection is people picking who will prosper (materially, at any rate, if only for a while) and who else will procreate, when we do so with our natures corrupted, desires unnatural, and instincts denied.

Natural selection rewards individuals and species. Unnatural selection rewards only individuals, and only some individuals at that.

Much of the selection individuals make is by our indifference to others. Unnatural selection began with the unnatural West's rejection of our race and heritage.

Unnatural selection does not end the struggle to survive. The struggle is simply in unnatural environments. Without biological differences to distinguish between people, human authorities invented new differences around work, wealth, and values.

Survival of the Richest

If there is to be evolution among white people, it will be moneyed evolution. Our prosperity has become not so much a matter of nature as a matter of money. Survival of the fittest means survival of the richest.

People without governments, families, or other benefactors to keep them need jobs. Those with a better chance of surviving are those that vary however slightly in a manner profitable to buyers and employers while remaining acceptable to our ideological keepers, rather than any physical or intellectual superiority. While other discrimination became wrong, we increasingly discriminated according to people's economic usefulness.

Earning income depends upon decisions by self-interested sellers and employers. Employers employ for themselves. Employees work for themselves. (When employees become unemployed, we are nothing at all.) Vendors want customers. Customers want service. Once in a while, their interests coincide.

Small businesses do everything big businesses do, but they do it more efficiently. Big businesses can be no less bureaucratic than government.

Western companies declared their employees to be their most valuable assets, perceiving people to be business resources: factors in the processes of production and consumption, cogs in other people's economies. Human resources departments came to call employees human capital, akin to financial and physical capital. The sense of belonging in a company is inversely proportional to the number of human resources personnel.

Employers weed out the unhealthy. Employees malingering or fundamentally unwell are managed away. Life and death become factors in a business risk matrix.

Good health (disabilities notwithstanding) could have remained intrinsic to the human condition, to survival in our new Western world, except that employee health means just enough to work. The threshold of good health is low.

If drugs can treat afflictions or their symptoms enough to keep people working, then they remain able-bodied. Employees do not recuperate at home if they can recuperate in a company workplace performing proverbial light duties, which health and safety laws allow, even expect, employers to find. Employees continue working for as long as they can still use a telephone or computer even if their spleens hang from their bellies, provided no blood spills on the floor.

Corporations as Secret Societies

Paying the most money, corporations are the most influential employers, pervasive marketers, and prolific buyers and sellers in markets of purchase and sale, but corporations do not really exist. They are legal fictions we created to carry on commerce.

All that really exist are people behind the wide veils: directors, executives, managers, and employees, normally hidden from view. Corporations are secret societies, about which people outside know little. Admission is by invitation only.

The pictures around company offices are of company business and occasionally nondescript employees. Production matters, not people.

Bank walls are bare. Money cannot be pictured, when there is too much to be counted in cash.

Within each big corporation is a plethora of ever more secret societies, never letting the people within get close and never trusting the people without. Normally concentric and ever shrinking in size, eventually they hone in upon directors. Even people inside corporations know little about them.

Few directors, executives, or managers inspire respect or devotion. Few even try.

Managers well versed in work and company values do not need proficiency in human sensitivities. We lost interest in them, beyond what others expect of us.

Within the caverns of production and supply, employees are neither managed nor led. They are punished or rewarded. We do not always assert what we want, if we know assertion would affect our jobs, remuneration, or promotions in ways we do not want.

Sometimes, we get it wrong. Like natural selection before it, unnatural selection can be cruel.

We need to adapt to survive, or so we believe. We adjust. We evolve.

Discrimination by Values

Employers pick and choose employees supposedly according to merit, but really according to whatever criteria they want. Without a culture of quality or discrimination, everything is a commodity of one form or another, including people.

We are commoditised according to work. Provided we achieve an acceptable threshold of ability, all workers within a category are pretty much alike. We are like barley, wheat, and other grains. There are no matters of merit, but only of price.

Our only other distinguishing features are values and character. We judge people by their values as we do not judge them by their physical or intellectual abilities. When values came to matter so much to the unnatural West that we based our decisions upon them, values became ideologies.

The diversity we promote does not reach to values. There is no tolerance of contradictory values.

Discrimination according to people's values and character is lawful. Values are a reason to discriminate between applicants for a job or promotion and to dismiss employees, as few bases for discrimination in Western employment still are.

Companies do not allow employees to determine company values. Company values determine their employees.

It makes company values like laws. Companies require not just employees to share their values but also major suppliers, calling them partners when they do.

Company values do not make anyone a better person, but they are not meant to make anyone better. They are meant to convince everyone we already are what the company brochures say we are.

They are company officers and employees marketing the

company and our supposed values and characters to investors, customers, and communities. They are executives, managers, and employees marketing ourselves to each other. Most of all, we market ourselves to ourselves.

Corporations as Cults

The unnatural West is fixated with values. We think they make morality and religion superfluous.

Around company sites and especially at company conferences, there came speeches, awards, signs, posters, and highly choreographed short films (with bouncy music and extensive camera changes) exhorting company values, inspiring employees and others to keep doing more to live by the company lore. Company values vary in the specifics between companies, but they all include words like respect, inclusion, value, and diversity. They laud people, relationships, community, and most importantly investors, customers, and employees.

Company films and magazine articles do not normally dwell upon individual employees. Company awards are often issued to teams rather than to individuals. Anything else risks creating status for individuals rather than a company and its vision and values.

Vision means seeing what is already there and what is not there but could be, with the wisdom to know the difference and ideally a means to redress it. Only people without vision need to keep insisting they have one.

Without religion anymore, companies became like cults, with every sense of ritual from old religions and other cultures. Competence and incompetence are less important than placing a hand on the employee heart and vowing aloud to implement our employer's vision and values, making personal commitments to perform actions that advance the company brand. There is, in short, a persistent underlying hysteria about company purpose and principle: our reasons for being. At any moment, someone speaking before a company conference could start speaking in tongues.

Tribalism becomes another management tool. Employees should all feel bonding with the whole of the company to which they belong, until they are fired.

Real Values

Words are economic tools no less than political ones, in this Age of Ideology. They define and refine companies. They define the people who work there: directors, executives, and employees alike. Language dictates perception, titles become self-fulfilling. None of it has to be true.

The values important to unnatural selection are not those espoused in carefully worded declarations, but those that people observe in the people in charge. For all their apparent differences, ruling cliques share an extraordinary consistency of values, completely estranged from the values they publicly pronounce.

Executives and employees effectively put aside from our minds the company values we feel compelled to declare but do not practice in favour of reality principles we do not declare but feel compelled to practice. Lying removes honesty from the values in play, from the values that might endure.

In spite of the fanfare, music, and imagery surrounding a variety of sweet words and phrases, there are only three real company values, never stated aloud. Nobody expresses them. No one publishes them on company computer sites or affixes them to office walls. They are not part of the company branding, but branding is not meant to be real.

The first two of our real company values are comply and conform. Compliance is a person doing what he or she is told to do. Conformity is doing it without needing to be told.

Those two are the same values in suburban schoolyards, under totalitarian regimes, and across much of the world. They are most ironic in our supposedly free West.

The third unstated company value is commit: the third C. It distinguishes our unnatural West from everything else, because the commitment is not to families, countries, races, ancestors, or God. It is to the company.

Compliance

Company values and branding are batons of righteousness to wield, but not upon people more senior. Employees and executives wanting to retain their jobs (let alone be promoted) do not challenge people senior to them about anything as important as their behaviour.

Enforcing rules against people junior to us but not people senior to us is perfectly ethical. The people senior to us expect it.

Company seniority has little to do with ability, physical prowess, or beauty. When decisions are theirs, directors invite new directors onto boards and elect chairmen they think will not confront them. Sometimes, they get it wrong.

Rarely are people with so little personal respect or affection for each other as collegiate as they can be on company boards. Even independent company chairmen know to do what more powerful people want them to do.

At the top is absolution. Chairmen of company boards are no more required to follow rules that executives lay down for employees than kings of old were required to follow rules that lords set down for their serfs. They do not need to contribute anything to enjoy absolution. Most of them do not.

When directors want a project to proceed, management's analysis need only justify the decision that directors will make anyway. Directors dismiss any analysis opposing the decision they desire.

Submission is everything. Provided chief executives are suitably subservient to their boards, according them whatever they desire, chief executives can do pretty much as they like. Provided managers are suitably subservient to their masters and mistresses, according them whatever they want, they can do pretty much as they like.

For good and for bad, chief executives ordinarily abandon office culture to their personal assistants. Secretaries enjoy the authority and almost the status of those executives to whom they report, as those executives want. No executive can overcome a personal assistant empowered by her managing director.

Executives carefully adopt company rules that do not limit them. Managers do not enforce rules that would limit them. Neither need comply with the dictates they make, but they keep their non-compliance discreet.

For all the hoopla of visions, company values, and branding, individual employees work for particular managers, as if they are in the manager's personal employ. In effect, they are. Managers are accountable for outcomes charged to them by chief executives.

Every employee within a division is the means by which that manager succeeds and employee fails. The results are the silos in which people work.

When employers recruit team players, they want people who do what they are told to do. Success demands we do what the powerful demand we do.

When powerful people politely say something could be done, they mean it should be done. Conversely, professionally educated people respond to orders much like they are requests (which they generously accommodate) and requests much like they are orders (unless they are willing to be dismissed).

Educated morons might prevail over uneducated morons, but company-compliant morons always prevail over independent-minded genii. No ideal candidate for a job (woman or man, childless or a parent) is anything but compliant.

We have become comfortable in compliance. Smart people know not to debate anything important. Smart people do not wage battles they will lose.

Compliance cascades. Daisy chains can be long, even if the daisies dwindle in size.

There is nothing necessarily wrong with dictatorship; it often works well in military units and film crews. Things come down to what the dictators do: their visions and values.

Conformity

Demanding diversity in everything else demands conformity in character and values. It is sameness in diversity.

The simplest and most obvious conformity is in grooming and dress. Fashion means the conformity changes, but in all cases we abandon our choices to others. Dressing otherwise can be arrogance, by people powerful enough to show they need not conform any more than they need to comply.

The powerful among each group sets its norms. Norms change.

Managers insist they do not want yes-people, who simply agree with everything they say. They want people who agree sincerely with everything they say, with all our heart, mind, and soul.

Whatever we happen to be and however we perceive ourselves to be, we recruit, retain, and reward people like us, in those features we consider important and so far as the law will allow. Conformity becomes feeling and thinking what more powerful people expect a person to feel and think, or seeming to anyway.

The diversity we laud rarely extends to matters of opinion. Diversity never extends to matters of opinion about powerful people.

Academia, media, and other professions become dominated by people with particular political views because they are chosen for those views. Ideologues care more than other people care about people's opinions. People without those opinions are excluded, removed, or learn to lie.

How hard or well people work is irrelevant. What matters are the opinions held by people in charge.

Employers are no longer looking for sane emotionally balanced employees. We appoint team-minded individuals eager to learn, work, and earn, from whom we remain comfortably apart. We still choose candidates for a job or promotion with whom we feel comfortable, but so individualistic have we become, we are not looking to become close to our colleagues.

Businesspeople no longer confront people and issues. Instead, we have become sneaky.

Personal conflict can be relationship, but the unnatural West no longer does relationship. We just leave the room.

Professionalism has come to mean working without complaint, no matter how badly a person is treated. Silence, and the isolation it brings, is the new professional etiquette.

Uncompromised by honesty, we best say how wonderful everything is. Employees see the way the wind blows, learning to recite values ruthlessly enforced. We say what powerful people demand we say, whatever we believe. We stand before audiences keenly lauding what we know we should laud.

Without real senses of being groups, the teams that companies vaunt are tools by which nominated team leaders and everyone else exercise their individual interests. Employees keep themselves for the most part to themselves: a secret universe, apart from everything they seem to their managers to be. Being tight unified units from adjacent offices and workstations does not mean people like each other. Our selves are each of us alone.

We should not be too friendly with our colleagues. Smiling lacks gravitas. We should be stand-offish, estranged from everyone.

Our companies become police states: corporate totalitarianism. Employees mistrust each other, expecting their words to be reported.

The challenge for employees becomes not letting the company know what the company ought not to know, but confiding in the company monitors whatever we would like the company to think. Free market economics is predicated on individual self-interest.

The closer the walls around people seated together, the stronger the pressures the group exert on each individual, the greater the compulsion to conform. Inside company meeting rooms, where profits obscure all other perspectives and executives focus so well on their jobs, even the kindest of executives can come to be callous.

Commitment

There was a time that our commerce served Western Civilisation. Without races and nations, we ceased using economies to improve Western lives. Western lives became means of improving economies.

We proudly reduce people to their contributions to commerce: their work and trade. Human populations matter by their economic impact upon us. It is all we perceive.

From a distance, people are pounds and pennies. Close by, they are ladders along our careers and anything else we desire, and hurdles obstructing us.

Employers like employees ingrained in their work. We regard anyone expending five hours to complete a task as inherently more dedicated than someone completing the task within two hours. Successful people are not those for whom work is merely an adjunct to life. They are those completely committed to their careers.

Time away from work is merely respite. Corporate hospitality has become slothfulness, unless it is a chance to further business objectives, or to pretend to further business objectives. We do not admit to lives beyond our careers.

No longer are we in jobs only while performing those functions, like we are pedestrians only when crossing the road. We are never unemployed, but between positions or consulting. Not merely the means of earning money, work became our identity. It is all we see when we look in the mirror and all we feel when we lie in our beds in the darkness of night. It affirms, defines, and becomes us.

We no longer have families. Instead, we have colleagues.

We no longer have communities. Instead, we have meetings.

We no longer have countries. Instead, we have workplaces.

Myopic worlds of half-floor offices consume our little lives. We are there to work, but not change. The more broad-minded of us might think of whole careers, but only ours.

We are no longer citizens. We are employees.

Not just satisfying but surpassing corporate expectations brings employees promotions. There are too many subordinates and too few managers for everyone to ascend.

Model employees hope merely to endure, creeping up a few management tiers through the course of their careers. To rise any further when the only people in sight already concede everything to their work, we need one extra trait: the one vision and value that managers never demand from others. If they recognise it, they reserve it deep to themselves, wary of sensing it in somebody else for what it might mean to them. Unique to our unnatural West, it is a willingness to condemn all life on earth to damnation, for the sake of one extra inch in the size of their offices.

The Countries Outside

All over the world, companies are microcosms of the countries outside. For all that Western companies do to shape the towns and cities outside, the towns and cities outside also shape Western companies. Unnatural selection is as much a Western phenomenon as a Western corporate dictate.

Western women might be choosing to pursue careers because they feel suitable, appealing, and available men are too few. Much like natural selection, women who feel they are least likely to secure a mate are more likely to choose career, to avoid the disappointment of wanting marriage but failing. They might feel they are unattractive to men, but it is a rare woman who is not beautiful when she smiles.

Women might also be pursuing careers because they feel they cannot rely upon men to keep them. Men might no longer be sufficiently financially resourced to appeal to women, or women might no longer feel they can rely upon men, as they could when their shared nationalism and other tribalism connected them. Yet it is a rare man who cannot provide for a woman when he tries his hardest to do so. It is a rare man who cannot befriend a woman when he is charming.

Men and women might be lulled into wanting something other than marriage. Every school and other pressure, except perhaps our parents and grandparents, push us elsewhere.

Lovers without Love

A man needs a woman. A woman needs a man.

Only the unnatural West thinks otherwise. We are individuals.

Western individualism means we can love and be loved but gladly live apart, convinced other people cost us integrity we think we each have alone. No one lies too long beside us through the night. Anyone with us in the morning should not assume it will happen again. We are rich enough not to share expenses, and too rich to risk our wealth with relationships.

Thinking we have everything we want, we might not call ourselves lonely but say we are comfortably alone, while everyone we meet remains a stranger. We sit in long conversations, plastering our faces with signs of people who care, until our knowledge of each other is less than the résumé we give when applying for a job.

We drive cars for one and cherish privacy as a right. We do not notice acquaintances not obstructing our way. We give money to beggars sitting on blankets, so our eyes never meet.

Reliant only upon ourselves, we might like our friends, but keep far enough apart to come back home alone, without anyone but us untidying our homes. Sitting in big houses or the spare rooms of our two-bedroom flats, our comfortable and uncomfortable abodes are spaces for work and our leisure, but none or too little for other people.

Social networking computer sites leave private people private. So does typing anonymous opinions into news sites for solitary strangers to read. A thousand absent friends listed on a bright computer screen does not leave a person less alone. Exhibitionism finds widening audiences, but we presume others are being truthful while we garnish our truths with lies we believe.

We talk about us to people we do not meet. We talk of other things to people we do meet.

Working hard becomes more comfortable than doing something more. Why experience the emotional uncertainties of loving another, when we can buy a fresh pair of shoes and choose when to discard it? Given a choice between a dear friend for life and a spanking new sound system, we are picking out the speakers.

We love ourselves too much and too little to love anyone else. Ours are rights to be alone, our intestinal solitude, without risk that anyone could emotionally touch or be touched by us. Keeping our secrets to ourselves, rarely dare we talk of love or chances we could. The depth love can be means we dare not risk our rapport by confessing whether we have loved, could love, or have ever been loved. Love might frighten our dear friends away.

He might have one long encounter he calls marriage or strings of encounters he calls relationships with women spun from his networks. She might be alone, in a relationship, or alone in a relationship; not yet lonely but alone, not loving anyone. Within a relationship, he might question whether staying is in his interest. She might not care enough to wonder. Mere time together is not reason to love.

Our loves are leisure pieces: lust and romance in recess times and holidays. No passion is for people. We believe lies people tell us so presume they believe our lies in return; those talking of love do not love anyone too much. Love is not supremely enduring or even profound for people passing through private moments of our lives, but safely confined by us to people who have died.

We love other people of the world enough to give everything to them, but the love we profess upon all people is a lyric bestowed upon none. We talk so much of loving everyone, but think too little of loving anyone.

We have made love what we want it to be. Giving money to charities might be generous, but generosity to people we have never met is hardly love. What we feel for other peoples, pets, and plants are not loves but chores: visions of our kindness or monstrous great guilt.

If they were love, we would love ourselves. We would value ourselves at least as much as we care for others. We would not let ourselves die but want to live, so we could love more and do more good. We would enjoy being in love, living love.

We might then derive scope to love someone we know; talk of a heart is no substitute for sharing it with someone nearby. Loving people like ourselves, our equivalents in that complementing gender, help us love ourselves. That love is not a superficial self-serving adulation, but the abiding lifelong love that expects manifestation in procreation. Love is too important to treat any other way.

Marriage

Across all tribes and races, although some more so than others, traditional morality focussed especially upon the interests of babies and children unable to assert their interests themselves. For babies and children, and thus for their tribes and races whose longevity depended upon there being babies and children, those tribes and races valued family structures.

Childbearing and raising are in society's interest. Thus, families are in society's interest.

Outside the unnatural West, marriage remains almost universal. Social status and acceptance depend, in large part, on being married and creating a new family, perpetuating two old families. People fear that unmarried men lack stakes in the social order, turning to criminal behaviour, thereby threatening societal stability and security.

The unnatural West does not care. Western parents do not let our children give us the stake in social order that children of other races give their parents. We are individuals, without social orders, societal stability, or security.

We have surrendered our tribes and races, so lose our rationale for valuing families. The unnatural West treats any social structure, unless it is political or economic, as being authoritarian for keeping us from our individual selves and preventing us from pursuing our individual wants. Individualism, no less than Marxism, is the end of marriage and family.

We have replaced our natural prejudices defending our peoples with unnatural prejudices against them. We laugh at jokes about husbands and wives, mothers and fathers, children and babies we would never accept about other races and cultures, not even their spouses and children. We mock marriage as we dare not mock multiculturalism.

Husbands and wives became nondescript partners to assert their equality and indistinguishability from unmarried boyfriends, girlfriends, fiancés, and fiancées, whether cohabitating or not. Disappearing into a bland sameness says nothing of gender or relationship, making a lover for life indistinguishable from another person playing bridge.

The more the unnatural West pursues inclusion, the more we exclude. Whenever the unnatural West pursues equality, we end up with nothingness.

We focus upon our individual feelings. Other races focus upon togetherness, making married couples more likely to see through hard times. Families are more than merely the sum of each individual.

We have come to see couples as separate from their families. Other races see couples as parts of extended families. Their marriages marry two families or extend at least one family.

Wives choosing not to take their husbands' family names are one thing. Retaining their maiden names for their careers keeps their careers separate from the rest of their lives, which might or might not be sensible.

Prohibiting wives from taking their husbands' family names is something else. It keeps them apart from their husbands, and their husbands apart from them. By asserting their different families of origin, they are keeping those families apart. At least to some degree, they are declining to coalesce into a couple and then a family of destination, exacerbating the solitariness around each of them.

Divorce

If individualism and the decline of Christianity do not deter us from marriage, they contribute to marriage breakdown. Believing in a perfect God encourages us to accept imperfect people and thus our imperfect spouses and marriage. We should never confuse a perfect God with imperfect Christians or an imperfect Church.

Without faith in God but blind faith in romantic films and television, white people presume their individual selves are close to perfect. They expect their spouses to be closer still, however horrible they think other people are. They are less tolerant of their spouses' imperfections than they are of other races, much as their spouses are intolerant of their imperfections.

Without tribes and races, the unnatural West has no reason for adults to defend the interests of babies and children. Determined to do whatever we individuals want to do, we do not let anything deter us from leaving our marriages. Thus, we insist that children do not suffer from their parents' separation and divorce.

It is not true, as many of those children will attest. Children of married couples develop better mentally and socially than the children of unmarried couples and single parents.

Rarely do we admit to the self-interest that compels our every behaviour. We do not want any knowledge about human nature that might diminish our self-centred but noble view of ourselves. Our excuse for not mentioning the harm children suffer by their parents' separation and divorce is not us but the children: we insist we do not want children stigmatised by the divorces we carry out regardless, as if a stigma is the children's primary concern.

Committing to marriages can be difficult knowing not just how easily our spouses can walk away, but how easily we can. Marriage vows might speak of commitments to remain married until death do us part, but remaining steadfastly individuals implies the proviso to our every commitment: for as long as we choose.

We have every right to depart a marriage, but no right to remain when our spouse is departing. We have rights to aloneness, but not a right to togetherness.

While Western laws enforce commercial agreements, we have made marriage the only commonplace contract between adults that is unenforceable: commitment without contract. Obtaining a divorce normally requires much the same paperwork as obtaining a bank loan.

We do not make commitments other people are not honouring anyway. The risk of divorce frightens some people from marriage altogether. Individualism is our insecurity.

Relationships become fickle. Good relationships falter. Where relationships are fragile, fertility suffers.

Fearing the people we call lovers will find others more beautiful and brilliant than we are, we are not confident we will not be parents alone. Conversely, we conjure a conceit that we will be the ones to find someone better. We do not want children holding us back.

The commitments we want are from others to us. We make commitments we must to secure them.

We should only make commitments we are willing to honour. Honouring commitments gives us certainty and structure, which is in our interests more than we individuals appreciate. The principle is never more valid than in relation to marriage.

If couples are not willing to be wedded for life, they should marry for whatever period they agree beforehand or should expressly agree they can each walk away upon whatever terms they approve. They would be bound by their vows, unless they both agree to amend them.

Like other contracts, innocent parties could divorce spouses fundamentally breaching a contract of marriage, such as by adultery, abuse, or refusal to parent. Either party could terminate the marriage for frustration, such as infertility. Children are intrinsic to marriage.

Parenthood

Human evolution does not depend upon individual evolution: individuals evolving within their lifetimes. It depends upon people becoming parents.

Before politics and economics mattered so much, one traditional adage said men cared about their children. Women cared about their and other children.

Every adult began life an infant in a crib, a vulnerable small boy or girl: somebody's child. Seeing other people in terms of their births and childhoods can make us nicer people. It is no reason to excuse wrongdoing or tolerate the intolerable in adults, but is cause to pause before rushing to hate them. It can make parents the nicest people.

When we had community, kindness, and contentment, men stood up for women. We all stood up for pregnant women.

Most proudly, women were homemakers and men their providers. A common compliment was to call a man a good family man. Nothing made our forebears prouder than the homes they made, families they kept.

Employers preferred to employ married men with children for being more complete, stable, and grounded than other men. We saw people with dependants, particularly children, to support as being more deserving of the privilege of income, often paying them more money than we paid bachelors. Thinking in terms of our nations and races, their children were our children: our futures.

Paid employment was necessary to provide income, but neither men nor women imagined there to be anything intrinsically wonderful about it. What were wonderful were the families we could raise with the income we acquired: the homes, beds, meals, and more, even holidays, especially holidays.

In the expectation of soon raising a family, women often retired from their jobs when they married wherever their husband's or parents' wealth allowed them, so as not to deny a job to someone who needed it. Later, many women retired from their jobs when they fell pregnant.

Nobody forced those women to retire from paid employment. They wanted to retire from that phase of their lives, because progressing to raising a family was natural. No husband begrudged his wife raising their children.

If we came to feel that society somehow pressured those women, it was because their collective sense of being a people gave them all interests in their children being born and raised well. That sense came most from other women, because social mores did.

If the West still saw the world of human beings and relationships instead of political power and commercial transactions, we would realise how matriarchal we were. When fathers became sick, family life continued. When mothers became sick, family life struggled.

Expectant mothers were great with child. Children took the religion of their mothers.

A woman is never more powerful than in becoming a mother. A man never stands taller than in becoming a father.

Women traditionally saw older women without children as being incomplete. Older men without children were strange or the victims of social or biological misfortune: obvious among the fathers at work because they did not talk of their children. Life was about marriage and marriage was about having children, saving money for the children's success.

Those times might return to the West but, for the moment,

amidst this Age of Individualism, they have passed. No longer are we societies embracing our compatriots' children as our own. We do not support women giving birth, their children, or the fathers of their children. We do not support them beforehand or afterwards, beyond what we must.

Western children are no longer born to their families, races, and nations (as those of other races remain born to theirs), but to individuals. Parenthood is consumption and parents are the customers: not the children, family, or race. Only individuals consume.

Devoted spouses and parents, to the extent they remain in the unnatural West, are only devoted to *their* spouses and children, nobody else's. The lives for which they want meaning are their own.

At best, our unnatural Western perspective avoids reference to people being parents or not. At worst, what once we encouraged, we banned.

The end of race and nation is the end of community. The end of community is less childbearing or, for many, the end of childbearing.

Promoting Childlessness

Childbearing is natural. Procreation is natural.

Rights are illusory. Powerful people mould their exercise by others. When we had races, nations, and families, women wanted prohibitions upon abortion to protect them from men pressuring them to abort their babies.

Since then, women in the unnatural West have lost much of their right to mother, but have gained quite a right to abort. In their pursuit of profit without regard for the impact upon others, abortion clinics in Britain drive the lie that abortions are safer than carrying babies. They suppress professional advice that rates of psychiatric illness and self-harm are higher in women who have had abortions than in other women.

Natural selection promotes procreation. Unnatural selection discourages it, at least among us. Deliberate childlessness is a political or social construct, denying people something of human nature.

The West supposedly ceased celebrating parenthood for fear of excluding people without children, but all we began doing was celebrating childlessness. We have the money to do so.

Unnatural selection promotes everything but parenthood. In our unnatural Western hierarchy, there is only money, materialism, and vocation. Rather than the marriage and children that drive most of the world, the unnatural West wants people to find satisfaction from careers, competing with other people's careers, and shopping. We exhort working and spending, rather than motherhood and fatherhood. We become what we want others to be.

We can do whatever we want to do, provided we want careers. We regard it as perfectly proper to carry out school programmes and advertising campaigns encouraging people to work, enter trades, or take apprenticeships. Encouraging people to join the armed forces can be a little controversial, among some people. Our schools, films, television, and news media promote careers for men and women, especially women, as they do not promote parenthood.

Unless we are selling disposable nappies and brand-name baby clothes (adding to costs people perceive in becoming parents), businesses would rather advertise their product than parenthood. There is not enough profit from parenthood for companies to want it; not soon enough anyway. Children without money are not customers.

Our natural desires wane a little more with each passing year. People content until the 1960s and '70s to work, raise children, and play without thinking much about it are no longer content.

If we do not dispense with children altogether, we consign our unlikely offspring to others. If we have not married someone to raise children we employ nannies to do so. Those nannies might be young, pretty, and white. They might be older of colour with children of their own far away, being raised by their husbands. Nannies are more compliant than fellow parents can be. They are also more readily dismissed.

We contract out child rearing and bearing. Being keen to remain working, and to avoid pain, epidurals, and inconvenience, surrogacy motherhood is a womb for hire. Without sense of race or nation, we believe everyone is the same anyway: commodity women with commodity wombs. The lease term is nine months.

Work is the priority. Ambitious employees rarely bear more than two children, one for each parent. Any more might intrude. They might bear just one, for the parents to share.

University-educated women increasingly have just one child each, if any, believing more parental attention helps their child succeed. It is a lonely sense of what constitutes success.

Ideally for each of us so much the individual, we might think we do not need a fellow parent to share the costs and chores of parenthood. We might think we can parent alone. Cloning offers replication without compromise.

Childless Diversity

With bearing children natural, people do not need a reason to be parents. We need reason not to be.

We think we have changed so much since the past, but if we changed to allow mothers in our workplaces, then we changed back again. Especially among women but also among men, employers want a certain kind of diversity: childless diversity.

Employees with families perform best in the office and parents make the best managers, but employers no longer want the best performers and managers. They want the most committed. Commitment makes someone best.

In our unnatural West, survival of the fittest means individuals seeing themselves solely as individuals, without families or races. Other individuals do not deter them from their pursuit of whatever they want.

Where compliance matters so much, babies can be singularly non-compliant. Many a Western businessman or woman expects children not to be seen, heard, or mentioned.

There is nothing more career-limiting than loyalty to our families. Western individualism erases every loyalty except those that corporate individualism demands: to more powerful managers. There is no place in our unnatural West for people to love or care for their spouses and children at the company's or their colleagues' inconvenience. Familial loyalty is incompatible with company values.

A logical and illogical consequence of Western individualism is to separate prosperity from procreation, at least among us.

Employers prefer childless candidates to those with children, with pregnant women the least desirable of all.

We learn to keep children secret if we want to remain employed. For all our talk of inclusion, we exclude parenthood.

For people whose lives are predicated upon careers more than achievement, motherhood and homemaking are not experience. To employers focused upon work they can extract, parenthood can be a failing.

Our careers are best served by being single and childless. We can then keep working. We can work extra hours. Commercial interests make childlessness compulsory.

Shortness might have been a problem for natural selection, but might be useful for its unnatural counterpart. Short men appear more likely to remain childless, for much the same reasons as they once were less likely to succeed.

At the most senior levels for most companies, diversity means diversity in gender. Merit does not enter into it, except perhaps between women.

We embrace women in our workplaces to work, disenfranchising them for profit from parenthood. In their pursuit of careers, women oblige.

Proud of being without discrimination, individuals would claim to be without gender, but many traits we exhibit and reward are essentially masculine. We are competitive, perceiving transactions in terms of winning and losing. The outcome matters nothing, not the pounds and the pence, the dollars and sense, nor the profit or product. We need to win to assert our existence, accountable not just for what we do but what we are. Relentless economic self-interest means economics becomes a person's ego.

Feminine traits concerned with relationships have been subsumed from the unnatural West. So has nurturing.

Suppressing emotion is often the last battle we wage with our natural selves. Expressing emotions, except for some the most masculine of anger, has become rare in the workplace.

We have made parenthood more difficult than it needs to be: labour without compensation or career. Our corporations have become contraceptives, to which we concede not just our lives but our futures.

Without our senses of race and religion to save us, free market economics empowers the people who would end Western childbearing. The children we bear not because of our circumstances, but in spite of them.

Barrenness

For much of the world, people raise children to keep them when they age, but not us. We do not give money to our parents, except for something in return, so cannot imagine our children supporting us, ushering money our way when we no longer earn. Feeling financially insecure in spite of all that we have, we let money keep us from parenting.

Wealthy Africans and Arabs see their riches as reasons to bear more children. Poor Africans and Arabs bear children nevertheless.

It has become commonplace in the unnatural West to say economic prosperity reduces birth rates, without mentioning that no birth rates have reduced more than ours. Unlike other races, we measure success by something other than parenthood, as if the only prosperity were material, individual, and immediate.

The unnatural West is supposedly becoming wealthier, but in any lasting sense, we are not prospering at all. If we measured riches by children as other races do, we would understand how poor we are.

Paradoxically, the richest of white people are the most conscious of what bearing children might cost; those with the most are the most determined to keep it. If we feel rich, we see children no less than we see everything else in monetary terms; not for us the relationship or mere immortality.

If we bear children then it is because the benefits to us outweigh the costs, the amusement outweighs the expense. Our children are leisure items much like any other. They are fashion accessories wheeled out for portraiture.

The rich among us would rather holiday than bear children. Having acquired more goods and services than we ever can use, we acquire still more. Embroiled in work, we hoard ornaments we have no time to see.

Our lives become a glut of almost everything, but children. We think we are pleasing ourselves, whiling away in the garden or lying in the bright hot solarium, while the wealth and resources that should have made us more fertile leave us barren.

We make our toys more important than us. They are too engrossing.

With economics unfettered, the human condition wanes. No blight from our ideologies is greater than the end of our child making. Our impersonal tenets are manifest, but we live too well to see what we have become. Our work and active leisure, items of manufacture and other people's service, conceal the barrenness within us.

Infanticide

Too many of us do just what we feel like doing: forsaking feelings for which we feel unprepared. That so many white people no longer feel the desire to be parents speaks less of the desire than it speaks of the West. The abnormal only becomes normal in an abnormal environment.

People deliberately not bearing children can still be good people. Sometimes, good people make mistakes.

The only reason for us not to bear children that might possibly be honourable is a concern about passing on genetic conditions. It is the honour at the core of eugenics, but the eugenics we came to condemn after the Holocaust when applied to others we came to apply to ourselves.

Abandoning nationalism and belittling religion did not have to mean the unnatural West trivialised families. Embracing commerce and ideology so completely meant we did.

Beyond any fears of trauma giving birth, white men and women share much the same reasons for not wanting to be parents. Individualism means we think our lives are just ours (and we have so much to do), instead of sharing our lives with our ancestors and descendants. We take ourselves too seriously.

Children in the house impinge upon us being the centres of our self-centred worlds; other lives might curtail our career or choice of hobby. Childless people claim they can do more with their lives without children, but they do not do anything that parents could not do, if parents wanted to do it.

We think fatherhood and motherhood are not glamorous, but meetings are. Our arbiters of fashion, style, and success set their terms without reference to children. Self-destructive slaves to other people's thoughts let us all go down.

Without respect for our forebears, and our parents being the people they are or were, parenthood becomes the spectre of being like our parents. Too few of us are bold enough to step back from our childhoods for the sake of ourselves. We let our relationships with our parents determine whether we bear children, as if we have no chance to do better. The parents that gave us the present we let determine whether we, and they, have futures.

None of the rules we apply to our dealings with other races, we apply to our thoughts of bearing children of our own. We focus on whatever good we imagine comes from racial and religious diversity, while talking only of the troubles of childbearing.

Parents who laugh that their child or children are too many make those children sad. Those children believe their parents, rather than think poorly of them. Their parents' cruelty becomes theirs when they too lie alone, condemned to die in homes too big for one.

To dislike children is to dislike people; every person was once a child. A person disliking children dislikes himself or herself.

People choosing not to bear children lack self-love. In spite of our self-absorption, the unnatural West lacks self-love.

Nothing is more natural than for people to think the human species is better for their families and races enduring. Only white people see means of making the world better *without* bearing children, even *by* not bearing children. Beyond a lack of self-love is self-hatred.

People who do not have children because they think it is a bad world into which to bring children express the despair at the core of the unnatural West. It also means surrendering as our forebears did not.

Economy without Empathy

The tenets of economics are all assumptions: that people exercising their individual interests try to maximise their happiness; or that they try to maximise their power. In competitions for seniority within corporations and without, people wanting happiness gave way to people wanting power: power without happiness. With power, comes happiness, for some.

Caring for our compatriots without good monetary reasons to do so would be nationalistic, but we do not do nations anymore. We are individuals.

Helping people is no longer the norm for people with advice to proffer. Without nations to enhance or races to aid (at least our own), we have little reason to think about people we know, let alone people we do not. Freedoms give our compatriots every chance to succeed, if they have our hunger to rise. People born without wealth are often harder than people born with wealth on those not working hard enough to succeed.

In our lives premised upon choice, we think our compatriots neither need nor warrant our help, unless we are being paid to help them. Helping people thus became a task reserved for an abundance of dedicated professionals, charging fees for their guidance. From the company's nominated mentors or career coaches we pay, we learn more self-reliance, maintaining our spaces apart.

No less for employees than for investors, businesses have become simply income, and retirement plans when we age. We might think money binds us together, but it is just another means of expressing our individual interests. So is employment.

Western employee benefits have become paternalistic, as if paternity were an insult. All employers promise employees is money. That is all employees expect: the cash to decide for ourselves what to buy. The unnatural West is about money. Jobs should be too.

Employment is simply a monetary transaction. Employees are human resources and resources cost money: human costs and perhaps a revenue item. Companies provide as little for employees as they can without spurring an employee exodus. That is the free market: economy without empathy.

People whose standard of living is already very good justify their mistreatment of others by their desire to improve their standard of living still further. They expect others to be the same, but with financial security, families, and communities excluded from their concept of standard of living, at least as regards other people.

Managers do not care about their subordinates fretting over how they will meet their next mortgage debt repayments, working long hours to keep jobs they do not like, or being fired. Neither should their fellow subordinates care.

We need only to fret about our financial predicaments, disappearing time on earth, and social isolation. That is individualism.

When the demands of their jobs and of people around them torment enough of the people around us, we accept that working-place norm. We do not think of a burden when most everyone seems equally afflicted, even if only a few feel the pain. It is simply our unnatural West. We know nothing else.

Solitary people foist solitude upon others. The unnatural West has become indifferent to white people's lives, including white children's lives, as is our right being individuals. To survive and succeed, we become self-reliant not simply because we want to be, but also because we need to be.

Stress

Without races and nations in which to stand, we are left vulnerable in many ways. In particular, individualism leaves us emotionally fragile.

The distinction between health for our unnatural West and real health is starkest in cases of stress. Stress causes a person's body to produce cortisol, which increases weight and damages nerve cells including brain neurons, particularly as a person ages. We become fat and stupid.

Working hard is not stressful. Stress is something else altogether.

For the rich and powerful, executive stress is choosing what luxury motor car to buy. With every next layer of management downwards and diminishing control over our lives, stress becomes more acute. Businesses deal with employee stress by not mentioning it.

Most stress that managers inflict is more reckless than deliberate or malicious. After giving instructions and information, most managerial communication becomes nagging.

There is no limit to the grand trivialities: the importance of unimportant things. Businesspeople are more likely to demand memoranda use the official company font than they are to demand that those memoranda make good business sense.

Employees who submit completely to their bosses are empowered to bully everyone else. Sophisticated bullies are unpredictable: sometimes kind, sometimes cruel. Often being nice only makes their worst moments of torment more hurtful.

Bullying elicits meagre obedience. When people putting their heads up find their faces slapped around often enough, they learn to lie low. That is self-interest. We nod, we smile, but we do not imagine and we do not create. What remains are small insurrections.

Corporations are the only asylums that impose more tests upon people before admitting them, than they impose before letting them flee. The rest of us do what we need to do to alleviate duress, as best as we can. We do nothing more.

Without financial security, there is nothing more stressful than the risk of being unemployed: of not working. Nothing unsettles employees more than seeing their colleagues fired for something other than faults; faults they can often remedy or avoid. Working hard and well but still being pushed aside affects people with feelings as it does not affect people without feelings, although people without feelings seem less likely to be pushed aside.

Without empathy or morality to affect our perspectives, being reluctant to fire people shows a lack of leadership. Equal opportunity means firing women and men with equal abandon. Models of indiscrimination in everything but character, values, and whatever else suits their individual interests, managers should treat people equally badly.

There is little, if any, correlation between what management experts profess managers should do and what managers actually do. Economic theory presumes that company executives want to maximise company profit, but dismissals often cost a company expertise, accumulated knowledge, and a small country's economy worth of termination payments and recruitment costs hiring their replacements. Profit maximisation is selective: a reason to pay lesser people less money when they go, but not a reason to keep them in the first place.

No real company interest is behind most dismissals. There are only individual interests (even if only the pleasure of firing people), but not those of people departing or their dependants.

Western workplaces have become dog-eat-dog worlds. We need to fight as relentlessly and ruthlessly to keep our jobs, as others fight trying to take our jobs from us. To survive, we become like the worst of others: tirelessly manipulating people in power.

Paranoia is an irrational fear, so our fear of people like us is not paranoid. Our fear of like-minded people is perfectly rational. They can be formidable foes.

People determined not to work with awful people can buy themselves farms. If we want to avoid dealing with awful people altogether, we can try subsistence farming.

Western men's sperm counts have fallen of late. Some women have become too stressed in their careers to fall pregnant. Work stress kills some people. It drives others to kill themselves.

Money cannot alleviate every distress. In an evolutionary sense, and in spite of whatever pride and glory we might pursue, our careers' only consequences are the children they keep us from bearing.

Sustainability

Childlessness is not just a result of the isolation by which Westerners live, but a cause of more isolation: a compounding solitude. Children were the fabrics by which parents, especially mothers, weaved communities. Without children, communities wither.

While the rest of the world works to live, we live to work. At best, many a manager focuses upon the next accounting date by which his performance is judged and her bonus determined. Chief executives fleet into companies, achieving quick results by stripping out employees and other costs. They leave before the disasters they have created are realised.

Politicians rarely look beyond the next periodic election dates by which they are judged. They will have retired before babies born today vote.

If we do not live to work, we live to spend. Consumers seldom see past the point of consumption, for that would be like watching our weight instead of savouring a chocolate profiterole. We like to do both.

When consumers look past the moment, it is normally no further than the date of our next credit card statements. In the long run, without sense of our descendants, we are all dead anyway.

Seizing opportunity, several industries have arisen around the principle of sustainability. We espouse environmental sustainability whenever doing so is profitable: selective sustainability.

Production of goods requires raw materials, much as farming requires fertile land. In perfect fruition, our economies could be immortal, but in the unnatural West, even immortality has to make good business sense.

When there is more money in it to do so, we shut down our businesses. We cease the cost of maintenance and repair to let our factories run down. We then import what we sell.

Were we a people, we would not run down our manufacturing capacity to then import, but we are not a people. Were we a people, destroying a popular asset would be self-destructive, but we are individuals.

Businesses close and dismantle old factories and plants before heritage laws protect those factories and plants. We demolish buildings to escape the costs even empty buildings can be. We destroy those that reflect a heritage we no longer feel is ours.

The unnatural West applies commercial principles to sustainability of people. Our solitary lives are, of course, worth much more than other solitary lives; we have no equality about that.

We buy the happiness so life's benefit satisfies its cost. Prolonging our lives might warrant any cost when we are old nearing death, if we still have capacity to spend. Until then, we focus too much on the moment to care so far ahead. Pleasures each day are worth more than pain many years onward. Our health is an issue only if it immediately affects us, however much our lifestyles eventually might kill us. The only pain that matters is pain that we feel today.

Without children, we have no reason to retire. Without anything else to do, we keep working. Other people's mortality is just another business opportunity.

When people die young, we lament the careers they could have had, presuming there is nothing more to life than the work people do, and nothing more to death than the work people would have done. Studies and work are no longer merely the most important facets of our lives. They have become Western lives.

If work is everything, then failure at work is failure at everything. It is a reason to die.

Without thought of marriage and children, being unable to decide upon a career equates to being unable to decide what to do with a life. It becomes another reason for people to suicide.

Life and Death

What defines us in our unnatural West is not our best job. It is our current job. That is the place from which we seek our next job.

We presume our time at work to be important, proud of our performance, but nothing changes because of anything we do. Among the few managers who cast impressions, too many, particularly at the most senior levels, wreak only anguish upon people near them. Some people increase economic output or improve services, but the output and services were already enough. Most working people could walk on wet sand without leaving footprints. Trying to change things became wrong.

We have no end of phrases to describe people's jobs and acronyms to conceal them, but jobs are poor indications of how interesting or important people are. Doctors and nurses save people's lives but only for a while, deferring their deaths. The closest they and midwives get to creating lives is helping parents create them.

People complaining about parenthood promote childlessness, presumably for the sake of reward: barrenness for fools wanting to believe them. Holed up in cabins in a forest, dying in anonymity, their aged trembling hands can clutch the last editions of their work, rotting in the damp. They will weep and wail for someone to bring them medicine, without anybody hearing. Strangers do not come to see loneliness through the years that people die, without being paid to do so.

We concede our days to make what does not really matter, letting ourselves expire to earn little bits long dead. Valuing promotions more than parenthood, we might well die old and rich.

We might die in the company of our computer terminals or alone while the nurses are in other rooms, watching their television sets or playing with their telephones. The closest networks of our friends might enjoy half a day of compassionate leave to attend a small service for our passing, if they can reschedule their appointments at the office or with their pedicurists. A recruiter might arrange our replacements, or the remaining staff might reconfigure their roles to take up what we did. No one need know that we have gone, and no one need know that we were there.

Company Histories

Without races and nations, we cannot call any people's history ours. History becomes an exercise in academic discourse, interest, or curiosity.

We have only personal histories. The history most likely to matter to us is our own. We call it a resume.

Second to that for businesspeople is not national, racial, or even family history. It is company history.

The company founder could have been a forebear, but still a family history means nothing. We no longer have families, but at least have their company names.

As it is with everything else, our imperatives are political and economic. If the unnatural West premised upon companies can seem fragile and brief, we concoct histories to make new companies seem old. In older industries, confidence among bankers and customers comes from carrying on business since 1892. In newer industries, confidence comes from trading since a week ago last Tuesday.

Publicly, powerful people talk of drawing upon great traditions. Privately, they gloat over all they have changed. Glorious pasts cajole people through disappearing futures.

When history does not serve present objectives, we shed it. Our new values make history superfluous at best. Being antiquated is a bigger insult than being called incompetent.

At worst, history threatens our new ethos. For anyone seeking real change, real history can really impede.

Records are better destroyed than retained. Maintaining them is a cost. Deleting them is easy. Laws normally require taxpayers and companies to keep only some records, and to keep them for only a small number of years.

Statutes of limitations encourage people and companies not already involved in litigation or pending litigation to discard records quickly. If a court order or government inquiry forces a person or company to produce its records, the last file in an old folder might be more likely to harm than to help. The plaintiff wanting to sue or prosecutor wanting to convict normally carries the onus of proof in the West, so where evidence is insufficient to ground a conclusion, the defendant or suspect most likely escapes culpability.

Even among the innocent, trawling through records can be costly and cumbersome. There is no trawling if those records do not exist.

Real history dispensed with, our unnatural West constructs new histories. Among the allocation of company responsibilities, human resources divisions normally create company histories.

We choose the history we want. What we do not choose, we create.

The purpose of history so crafted is not to record facts, but to serve management's present objectives. We lambast past managers and owners when we want to make us look better.

We lambast past values to call our new values much better. Values matter more, much more, than facts in our ideological West.

Erasing real history requires erasing people who were there. The easiest way to change the culture of an organisation is to change the people. The same could be said of a country.

Fertility Ghettoes

Human evolution and devolution do not depend simply upon people becoming parents. They depend upon which people become parents.

Without being a society, we drive parents to exile. Childbearing and rearing are contracted away from swanky offices, shops, and homes to fertility ghettoes, where the rest of us do not think about them. If those strongest and most intelligent people that companies do not hire were among them, then the processes of corporate recruitment and retention might not matter so much, but they are in professions where their customers demand they be available and in universities with too much else on their minds.

Western governments are no more natural than Western corporations. While many governments provide financial assistance to parents, they discriminate only on the basis of money, as the unnatural West does. They might impose income and other means tests, but not intelligence, character, or physical tests. That would be discriminatory.

When governments prioritise government housing to parents with children and parents with the most children, they invite people to procreate for somewhere better to live. Parenthood can seem a lot easier than study and work, for people without the intelligence or character to make much of either.

Government assistance to parents risks making parenthood a job like any other, albeit for many a temporary assignment. For people to bear children for money, the income to procreate must be their best income available. The smartest and healthiest of people forgo too much income through periods of confinement for mere subsidies to entice, except at the margins of decision.

Even if parents receive their usual remuneration through periods of parental leave, we fear that our careers suffer, in an unnatural West where parenthood is not the experience that employers want from employees. It lacks commitment to career.

We simply take the money for raising children we would have raised anyway. We are not trying to sustain our families and race, any more than Western governments or corporations are.

What makes Western selection most unnatural is that we are picking others, not us, to procreate. The people we do not risk losing are the people we rarely see. Parenthood persists among people we want tending to stores and eateries, cleaning offices and high streets, and collecting garbage.

Parenthood also persists among the people we never see: our subservient underclass. Unnatural selection propagates people natural selection might abandon.

While we decline to bear children for their careers and other reasons, people of most other races prefer to bear them. They might be materially poorer than we are in their fertility ghettoes around Western countries.

They might be materially richer than we are in their countries or ours. Unlike us so involved in our jobs, people of other races do not work at the expense of their families and races. Their work expresses their families and races. It feeds, clothes, and otherwise supports their families, much as our work used to support ours.

The unnatural West expects education for vocation, along with mass marketing, to dictate the values of commodity children. The weakest and stupidest of people can still become employees and consumers. We might even prefer employees and consumers like that.

Our wealth and other attributes do not condemn us because we let them fail to save us. Our work and characters might be the wondrous world we want to make, but they are jobs and characters for nothing without people to enjoy them. Causes do not exist without people to profess them. No principles survive when principles bring us down. Ideals and ideologies hardly matter.

By our work and wealth, we are trying to procreate our values and character, even our economies, but people are not commodities. We can be brilliant, magnificent, the most wondrous people of earth, but childless we die.

We take crazy things too seriously, when the world and being alive are ours to relish. The most beautiful and bright give up their lives to keep trivialities intact.

Wealth lies not in gold or money, but in warm flesh and blood. Whatever we might think of them, sweeping the floor while we bustle along past them, people with children are rich.

Power lies not in names or technologies, but human beings and bodies. The lazy, stupid, and corrupt prosper if they bear children.

We have no thought of racial futures, but the future will be theirs in one all-conquering regard. Empires of people prevail over empires left without them.

We are uncompromising commercialists, driving ourselves to extinction. Other races do not need us to survive, but we can have confidence in other people only until we are not people anymore.

Happiness

Instead of corrupting human beings to suit economies, we could found economies upon human beings. The concept might seem radical, even ridiculous, but the West did not used to think so. Other races still do not.

Our curse is not economics, but the lack of much more. Friends and family are major contributors to personal happiness, along with health and work. People with children and jobs are more likely to be satisfied with their lives than those with fewer commitments, although satisfaction dips among people in their late thirties and forties trying to balance those commitments. What might seem like a sacrifice to a mere individual is not to a family or race.

As horrible to each other as individuals are, aging childless individuals are worst. While the childless build their little doll empires, parents go home to their families. Married parents, especially women, are more likely to report their lives have an important purpose than do their peers without children.

Mothers are the happiest people. Childless women are the least happy.

Commercial advertising never says so, but children save us money. They entertain us for hours without the ticket costs of lesser shows, delighting us more than we had thought they could. They introduce us to people we would otherwise not meet and to places we would otherwise not see. Not wasting time away from them frees us to enjoy more time with them, doing things we would otherwise not do.

Our children do not just teach us new waves in slang and how to use and circumvent the most modern technologies. Children make life's pitfalls easier to bear for having a family to ground us. They moderate us when we think too well of ourselves. They console us when we think too poorly. Only children quick to put us in our place provide balance and proportion to our lives.

For men and women, there is no greater pride than the pride to feel making a family home. If we marketed parenthood as well as we market products for sale, then we would all want to be mothers and fathers.

Our economies could be correct, if we live for the minute instead of the moment, if we live for all our family's lives instead of single instants in ours. The happiness we maximise could include the love we feel and the happiness of our families, sharing joys and successes, instead of merely things that we buy and we do.

Instead of buying a pocket digital device, personal fulfilment would be raising our people. Instead of buying a new kettle, happiness would be seeing our children smile.

We could custom businesses operated by good family men and women, among the criteria to consider. Laws grounded in the popular interest would allow employers to favour job applicants and employees with children or children to come. Nationalism would inspire those employers to do so.

Companies are unimportant, although an accommodating company might save a man as much as a cruel company can kill him. If a corporation is to be anything worthwhile, it would be a grandparent.

For all the banter around offices, few people say very much. The less we speak of what is important, the more we speak of what is not.

When we do not need to talk about work, we could instead ask and talk about people. We could talk about children and grandchildren, not just our own: how nice they are to see; how comforting they can be. We hear too little from those of us knowing that parenthood is the greatest, most profound, and important achievement of our lives. It is also much easier than any university course or professional career. Honest words can encourage people to bear children as effectively as dishonest words have discouraged people from doing so.

More telling than regulation is inspiration. If anyone mothers or fathers a child because of anything we say or do, then that child would be the greatest achievement of our careers. It might not seem very much, but none of our colleagues achieve anything more.

Immortality

As we age, the lures vocational guidance counsellors held before us in our youths no longer beckon. If people capable of doing a job do it and people incapable of doing a job teach it, or write books about it, then people incapable of doing any job become vocational guidance counsellors.

Even love and marriage are not quite enough, without children. People without children are poor, more worthy of sympathy than respect.

Infertility is mortality. If we let ourselves grow old without being fathers and mothers, then we have done nothing. All our reasons not to bear children, are fearful of bearing children, are foolish, when so few of us remain. To face death monetarily rich and nothing else would be bitterly dissatisfying. Childless lives that people call great are sick jokes upon themselves.

Without other immortality, our only future is the future our children make. Children offer immortality.

Our last heroines and heroes are women and men who, in spite of every pressure upon them in this unnatural West, bear us a future. Each person loving life enough to bring a child onto the earth, meaning to do the best by him or her, saves the world.

Whatever else we do or do not do does not matter, provided somewhere along our lives' long paths, we become parents, perpetuating our people beyond our deaths. Every other achievement, success, and all else we do is dust across the ground aside our sons and daughters, continuing or reviving the glory. What parents do is the most important thing we do, we joyous noblemen and women great merely for doing what is natural.

With a culture of children, the children we were and children we produce, we prosper. We are our greatest riches.

The unnatural West makes material considerations like the size of our house or car determinants as to whether we bring another child of ours into this world, but parents can give their children no greater gift than siblings. The more children, the better: each one is a life, with hopes and fears, joys and sorrows.

Only people are truly here: men and women with traits and nuances; boys and girls with dreams and gentle prayers. We each have one life on earth, our family one, our people one. We could value ourselves at least as much as we value our new values, our new views of everything, we starlets in doomsday. Only life is important, our lives.

The human experiences we have become unwilling to touch are not just those involved with the beginning of life, but also the end. We so often presume there will be a next time to see someone or do something, until suddenly there was only a last time we could have done so.

The lives that parents leave behind are not just their children. They are their grandchildren and so forth forever that natural and unnatural selection allow. Loving parents cannot really relax until their children are securely married and parents, too.

Few places are more challenging and more inspirational to explore than cemeteries. We do well to imagine what might be said or written about us after we die, if anything. Lives, even long lives, need not necessarily have consequence.

If our epitaphs are that we are grandparents, we will lie inside the soil more content than anyone with causes or career. Rewards richer than all others, we will have perpetuity.

3. THE NEED FOR NATIONS

Centuries ago, European peoples built the West's economic power, although it has become commonplace to talk of other races contributing out of all proportion to the facts. We did so with our labour, ingenuity, and co-operation. That co-operation was nationalism or other tribalism.

Having become disengaged from race and culture but immersed in politics and economics, we now think capitalism and free markets produce goods and services. They do not. Economic systems, like capitalism, communism, and socialism, do not produce or destroy anything. People do. The same economic systems that facilitate economic growth among some races fail to facilitate it among others.

Economic systems are simply descriptions of the rules and patterns by which people act, individually and collectively. Some systems encourage, others discourage. Some are efficient, others wasteful. Thus the same race adopting different economic systems at different times and places produce different outcomes.

It is the same with nationalism. All the nationalism imaginable cannot make some races rich.

Nor should we blame nationalism for war. Only people make war. Nationalism facilitates peace more than we appreciated in 1945.

For all the focus we give economics, ideological considerations matter more to the unnatural West than economic considerations. Without economic reason or justification, the West's rejection of economic nationalism since World War II has been our rejection of nationalism.

Co-Operation

To the puzzlement of Charles Darwin, evolution naturally favours those who co-operate over those who do not. Nationalism, racism, and other tribalism prevail over individualism. The tribes are triumphant.

Nature is tribal. The West no longer is, not for anything important. We have expelled our innate tribal feelings and think we are noble for doing so, but nationalism and other tribalism are not just natural. They are desirable.

When we had races, nations, and collective religion, employers kept employees in work. Employees worked. Rich people aided poor people, each respecting the other where respect was due.

White people no longer conceive of co-operating with each other as other races do, assisting each other instead of everyone else. Supporting each other became an anathema to us. That would be racist.

We presume much from believing we are individuals separate from each other. We are wrong. We need each other more than we understand.

Some degree of co-operation between people we know we need. With only the skills that earn us money in our specialised economies, no one person's skills suffice. We pay others to perform tasks we cannot or will not perform.

The most daunting of problems are more likely to be solvable by the cumulative wisdom of groups of people than by individuals. Some solutions require families, nations, and races. Shared interests can save us.

Ours is the great paradox among paradoxes. Individualism is against our self-interests, most obviously as individuals. Selfish people succeed by co-operating with other selfish people. A fixation with our individual self-interest is to our material and other detriment.

Globalisation

There is no end of irony to hear people lambaste the last remnants of Western nationalism for being narrow-minded. Tribes being just that, nationalism arose centuries ago when our villages, city states, and regions (not to mention aristocratic and merchant self-interests) seemed narrow-minded. We came together in nations and races, with national and popular interests supplementing individual interests. Through the twentieth century, the West replaced nationalism with the narrowest of all mindedness: individualism.

Nationalism is not narrow or isolationist. With the confidence of nations behind us, nationalism empowers us to go forth, while individuals remain preoccupied with their individual selves.

Countries outside the West are not booming merely by their own actions, but by a global economic model that pits Western individuals against other people's nations. Economic nationalism prevails over economic individualism, because nationalism prevails over individualism.

Nations have more resources to call upon than do mere individuals. They are bigger and richer.

Individualism fails because individuals are small, whether in fine homes with deep principles or in caravans with broken wheels. Our individualism leaves us weaker than we thought we would be: vulnerable to everyone else.

No matter how much smarter, stronger, or richer an individual might be over another, the cumulative capacities of races and nations exceed those of individuals. A stupid, weak, and poor population prevails over wise, robust, and wealthy individuals by the force of numbers, the weight of so many: the rule of nations. A solitary person, however brilliant and able, is no match for a mob.

Tribalism is only a problem for people without a tribe. Nationalism is only a problem for people without a nation. The world is no place for individuals.

Everything a single man or woman achieves alone is minute against what nations achieve. A person could stand atop all the riches he or she desires and that is all there is. They are meagre aside what nations enjoy.

The Sale of Nations

Classical economics presumed nationalism. In his 1776 seminal work *An Inquiry into the Nature and Causes of the Wealth of Nations*, Scottish political economist Adam Smith wrote of self-interested individuals in the context of nations. Vendors selling for themselves, consumers buying for themselves, and so forth maximised their and their nation's economic well-being. Invisible hands inadvertently helped all the self-interested people get richer.

Western individualism is unlike anything classical Western

economics contemplated. Two centuries after Smith died in 1790 with the wealth of nations, the unnatural West took up the sale of nations.

The unnatural West thinks we are better off without nations, but our forebears felt richer for them, at least until the Great War. The rest of the world feels richer with theirs.

Individualism leaves the West unable to deal economically or politically with nations. We are enriching everyone else.

Classical theories of free trade did not imagine us selling our inheritances: the countries our forebears built and died defending on our collective behalf. We trade territory, our fortunes stored in soil, in return for buying tiddlywinks we do not want and resin shelf-ornaments we soon discard.

We are exporting our countries so we can buy manufactured products instead of manufacturing them ourselves. We have ten times as many toasters but they are quickly falling apart, so we buy them twenty times more often, but only for as long as we have land and other assets to sell. The unnatural West sells our countries to foreigners at our descendants' expense.

Nor did classical economic theory contemplate nations buying so much on credit. Racking up debt defers the sale of our countries until payment is due. The free market forces that once redressed economic imbalances no longer do.

Holding Wealth

Within the West, some generations work harder than others work. Some save money, others do not. We save money if we fear poverty ahead, but fear less without having experienced economic recession. The unnatural West responds to all sorts of shocks with great manner of prudence, for a very short time.

We should stash wealth for when financial catastrophe threatens us. Banks and businesses sometimes fail, but financial security is some security nevertheless. We can value our home, health, and education, but nothing offers more financial and other security than a country.

Fundamentally, individualism is nihilistic and futureless. Our unnatural West feels little desire for saving (except to earn interest or minimise tax), only spending.

Western individualism creates opportunities for others. While the unnatural West stagnates, or fuels economic activity with asset sales or mounting debt, countries with their economic nationalism are becoming richer. Nationalist countries build national champions.

The people prospering retain their political, economic, and other nationalism, thriving with their countries even if they no longer live there. We wallow without realising it, holding fast to our economic idealism, rarely wavering from our individualist purity. We call it teaching as if by some divine example we are grand purveyors of wisdom and righteousness.

We have spent decades nagging the rest of the world to be like us. They care enough for their races and cultures, their ancestors and descendants, to refuse.

The rest of the world wants Western money, but not Western political and economic individualism. It wants nationalism.

The West could do what the rest of the world does, restoring the framework in which Adam Smith wrote. In simple terms, we could revive our economic borders.

Outside the unnatural West, countries prohibit or limit foreigners buying land and other capital assets. Others, to which few of us go anyway, would deny us before we bought huge tracts like those that foreigners buy from us.

We could do the same. We might allow foreigners leases, retaining the wealth our forebears entrusted to us to share with our shared descendants. At the least, we could restrict sales of land to countries that allow the same sales to us.

Those nations with gluts of foreign currency are buying the West and bits elsewhere, in a new era of empire: the empires to buy. They buy farms before needing the food. They buy territory.

Fertile land feeds people year after year. Infertile land is land nevertheless.

They are expanding their empires, not just at the West's expense. We are divesting.

There is nothing Western individuals will not sell for the sake of enough money. The West has lost sight of the value of what we possess.

Western economies still build empires, but those empires are no longer ours. We are the globalists, hopelessly individual, succumbing to other peoples' empires. Economic imperialism from their imperial homelands means that our countries become the subsidiaries of others.

Economic Individualism

Capitalism need not be individualism. It was not for the West until after World War II, well after.

Upon seeing a nice car or house, there are four types of people who want it. Some work to buy it, making their country more prosperous. That is, effectively, economic nationalism.

Economic nationalism means wanting to be richer, if material riches we want, without begrudging our compatriots their riches. It means working and letting our compatriots work.

Other types of people want to destroy that nice car or house so no one can have it, making their country poorer. Others still will try to steal it or will expect the government or others to give it to them, which would enrich them but impoverish their victim or donor, even if their country is no poorer or richer, until there are no victims or donors anymore. Each of those three latter responses is no less economic individualism for being socialist or communist.

Economic individualism, as much as socialism or communism, is a person wanting to be richer at the expense of his or her compatriots. It might or might not entail a person working.

Through much of the Cold War, the craziness of communism constrained Western capitalism from excess. Democratic governments wanted to keep the hearts of the people on side.

During the 1980s, Margaret Thatcher's Britain might have been the last remnants of British nationalism in political respects, at least for a while, but not in economic respects. She led Anglo-Saxon countries and thence the free West in our charge of economic individualism.

Governments invited private companies to take on projects that governments had previously reserved for themselves. They ripped away regulations. Neither would have been a problem if people retained their economic nationalism, but with much the same stratum of people running government and industry, they charged together.

Without nationalism, national corporations are no better than multinational corporations. Western capitalism became individualist capitalism.

Governments set the pace of economic liberalisation to whatever brought and kept them in power; politicians wanted jobs and were as susceptible to good marketing as was everyone else. Governments close to organised labour deregulated financial markets: the freedom to finance. Governments close to organised finance deregulated labour markets: the freedom to fire. Reform rarely meant anything but freer and freer free markets: economic individualism more and more.

Individualism is no less individualism for being bureaucratic. The European Union is not a European economy any more than the economy of any Western country is an economy of that race, with businesses wanting immigrants and establishing factories outside Europe. It is at least as much an economy for Chinese textile firms in Italy and other races within the European Union's economic borders.

Everything is economic in the unnatural West: the economics of individuals. The unnatural West exists for the benefit of people within no more than people without; we do not discriminate. Favouring poor white people working in Western factories ahead of foreigners willing to work in Western or foreign factories would be economic racism.

Western corporations employ rich people in rich countries and poor people from poor countries. Rich people in rich countries get richer. Poor people in rich countries become poorer.

Within the unnatural West, individualism accentuates inequality. Rich and powerful people object to economic nationalism for the West because they do not want any fetters upon their personal greed, while poor people suffer.

Individuals do not care if other countries rise at their country's expense, provided they collect and spend money on the way. Individualists care no more what happens to our countries than we care what happens to each other. We are not about to rein in the markets we equate with our wealth or people with money to spend however much people suffer, particularly if we are personally not suffering, not yet.

It is not so much that Western governments manage our countries poorly. We do not manage them at all. That would be nationalism.

Time

Nationalism and other tribalism draw people's attention beyond this coming Friday to the future. It is reason to care what happens to our descendants. Races, nations, and empires think forever.

Individuals think for the moment. We do not worry about economic futures any more than we worry about other futures.

While races and nations offer eternity, individualism confines us to one life, so relentlessly long and frustratingly short. Our self-interest is born of a moment and dies there, impoverishing us. We have no time to wait.

Patience was a virtue for Christians. In our unnatural West, it is a vice. It lacks hunger and greed.

We are rarely more miserable than when being forced to wait. Conversely, we keep others waiting when we suffer no cost in doing so.

Clocks are rarely far from us. More than merely ornamental, they are the measure of punctuality in everything not yet done. Impatient to do whatever we want to do, we have the right to be rude.

Maximising immediate profit demands urgency; our impatience brings forward our next task to whenever our current task finishes. Managers and clients who cannot assess the quality of our work judge us by the expedition of our performance. We do the same of others.

We treat anything today as intrinsically more valuable than anything tomorrow. We borrow money to buy goods and services before we earn money to pay for them, in spite of the fees and interest charged upon us for doing so. Anything years from now is practically worthless.

In the choices between money today and any kind of future, we are counting today. We cannot wait to mine and sell all we have, but extracting natural resources from below ground does not necessarily create wealth. It transfers wealth from one form to another, but normally can only do so once.

Races and nations are patient. China maintains its mineral resources for the time when resources will be hard to obtain, while extracting the rest of the world's resources.

Having become individuals, we are not interested in where it all leads, or anything else about the lives we leave behind: the problems more for later generations than ours. Ours is the pending poverty of individualism.

Economic Nationalism

Free market economics works. It works outside the West too, where people still practice a nationalist capitalism. Whether countries are democratic or dictatorships, with private or state capitalism, races collaborate among their own, wherever they live and whatever their citizenship.

Economic nationalism, like other nationalism, means pooling individual interests to a common benefit. Combining personal interests make for a public interest at stake. Countries offer common interests.

Chinese, Japanese, Jews, and other successful races are not more intelligent than we are. Many of them work hard, many do not. Their success arises because they support their own. In the empires of offices, shops, and cafeterias, each man and woman becomes a soldier in a job.

Much as they are for other races, collective interests would be in our individual interests too, provided our compatriots come aboard. Economic nationalism would be in our individual interests for the same reasons that nationalism would be. We would have people to help us.

Nationalism protects people not as rich as the richest, but not simply the poor and weak fare better with compatriots supporting each other. So do the rich and powerful.

There is much to gain by us suspending competition with our compatriots. Nationalism offers respite from global competition, which individuals jousting forever with everyone else are not afforded.

A Chinese, Japanese, or Arab might expend an extra yuan, yen, or riyal transacting with a compatriot, but earn that extra yuan, yen, or riyal from another compatriot's transaction. Economic nationalism gives them and their compatriots more chances to be rich.

Economic tribalism is economic nationalism. They work best among relatives, be they families, clans, or races. They fail between people without natural linkages. Co-operation requires commonality.

Government Nationalism

We had our moments of moderation. In 1982, President Ronald Reagan imposed a quota on sugar imports to protect American cane growers. In 1983, he increased the tariff on imported heavyweight motorcycles tenfold to forty-five percent, to save the iconic Harley-Davidson Motor Company in Milwaukee. Soon enough, such economic nationalism became unimaginable, if not illegal, in the unnatural West.

Government boosts for tourism are economic nationalism. If the Waterford City Council can support the Waterford crystal factory allowing it to reopen in 2010 for being a tourist attraction, knowing that tourists to the factory also spend money elsewhere in Waterford, then Western governments can support factories that are not tourist attractions, knowing that other businesses also benefit.

Like countries outside the West, Western governments could control large money flows and borrowing. Japan has its challenges, but the Japanese government owes its debt to Japanese people secure in their island home, as Western debt used to be owed to Westerners. It minimises their national vulnerability. They control their destiny, as Western countries no longer control ours.

The Euro currency made no sense economically, but perfect sense politically as a driver towards globalism: the erasure of European nations and even Europe altogether. Instead, Europeans could return to their national currencies, allowing their governments, people, and industries to shape their economies and determine their destinies.

Economic nationalism probably does not warrant currency fixing of the kind that China maintains, but it might. Currency controls might promote sales and deter imports.

Even while operating huge trade surpluses, China maintains relatively high tariffs upon consumer goods. It imposes sales taxes at customs, where slow and complicated procedures further deter importers. Restrictive certification requirements demand disclosure of confidential product information to supply critical infrastructure, preventing imports competing with local industry. China protects most of its economy from foreign competition altogether.

Other countries outside the West also assert their national interests, but everything about China, Incorporated is more obvious. We complain about China exercising its national interest (but not so loudly as to affect our business opportunities), as if China should not because we do not defend ours. We exert only individual interests.

Restoring Discrimination

People of other races customise businesses within their race when it is practicable, and often when it is not, although the effect is other businesses missing out on sales. Even in the unnatural West, such discrimination remains legal. Customers discriminate.

Immigrants also engage in employment and other discrimination which is illegal. Us noticing, let alone complaining, would be racist.

There are sound business reasons why employers would discriminate in favour of particular races, which necessitate discrimination against others. Service providers employ people of a particular race to serve customers of that race, especially in places where that race predominate, although nobody imagines employing white people to serve white customers. We are not pandering to racists.

Our Western sense of a single world is of a single world economy, but economic globalism is destined to fail because there is no single world economy. Nor are there multiracial economies, because there is little co-operation across races. There are only parallel economies of races co-operating with their own.

With identity comes money. The more opportunities people have to deal with their race, the more they do.

In 2020, Britain held her first Black Pound Day. Shoppers were to spend money at black-owned businesses.

White people do not object to other races' nationalism as we object to our own. We too could spend money at black-owned businesses.

People transact where necessary or desirable with people from other economies and with individuals not enjoying their own economies. Those transactions are often less co-operative.

Left to fare alone, white people lack economies of our own. We are individuals making individual transactions, oblivious to other races co-operating with their own: discriminating.

With the unnatural West leaving so much of our lives to free markets, we could leave discrimination to free markets too. We could let employers, suppliers, and landlords decide whether to discriminate on whatever grounds they choose. We could discriminate as other races do.

Employers might want the cohesion that comes from employing their own. Workplaces are more pleasurable and efficient with senses of co-operative community, excluding anyone who managers envisage disrupting the team. If workplaces are going to be tribal, with some chance for collegiality, we cannot compel them to be individualistic.

Cohesive workforces are racially and, generally, religiously homogenous. By banning racial and religious discrimination, we deny people those loyalties.

Prohibiting discrimination also prohibits any assessment of differences between races and religious cultures. Saying there are not any differences does not mean there are not any differences.

Employers, suppliers, and landlords should be free to decide what percentage of problem people from a particular race, culture, lifestyle, or anything else warrants discrimination. If they get it wrong, then in a competitive marketplace, they lose. For white people refusing to recognise differences, every person from a particular race, culture, or lifestyle causing problems making them commercially unviable would not be enough.

Even if no one from a particular race, culture, or lifestyle is a problem, liberty commands that people should be free to employ whomever they want to employ. Free people providing goods or services (except perhaps monopoly providers) should not be compelled to provide goods or services to anyone.

People of one race, culture, or lifestyle should be as free to discriminate against people of another as people of that other should be free to discriminate against them. That would not be individualism, but it would be equality.

Wealth and Happiness

Nationalism means the measure of national wealth is not the wealth of the richest among a citizenry or even some statistical median or mean. It is the wealth of the poorest.

Poor nations acquiring food, clothing, and shelter become happier because people become assured they have the necessities of life. Increased income thereafter reduces the sense of well-being if the social costs incurred to achieve it are too great. Rapidly growing countries are less happy than countries with slower growth rates.

Western economies have grown since the middle of the twentieth century, without any measurable increase in our happiness, but many things have happened through that time. Increasing wealth might have made us happier, had the wealth been applied to our betterment instead of bettering other races.

The West has become more unequal, but inequality has not reduced happiness, not among the rich. Amidst our economic individualism, it is not enough to be rich. We want to be richer than the people around us.

Wealth makes us happier if we are at least as wealthy as the people we know, while the inequities against us cause us pain. We complain about our compatriots richer than we are, but not about foreigners richer than all of us: the antithesis of economic nationalism.

Enjoying being rich or complaining about being poor, the happiness we want is our own. That is individualism.

Economic Growth

The most obvious expression of Western individualism is our preoccupation with commerce. Immersed in our world of data and lists, all that matters is an artificial construct of numbers called an economy, not a people, civilisation, or quality of life.

The West no longer sees races or nations. We see markets.

We no longer have cultures. We have economies. Without countries or cultures to grow, we grow economies, if we grow anything.

Esoteric masses of indeterminate people willing to buy or sell we call markets. Our glorious markets for purchase are all over the place: in homes and factories, schools and offices. At every point of our lives, through our work, shopping, and sleep, we are members of thousands or more markets. We are markets for socks we should probably buy and shoe shines we might possibly want. Bald men might be in the market to buy hairbrushes or even frilly nightwear, for the chance they buy one for a gift.

We speak of markets much as other races speak of races and nations, with interests, objectives, and knowledge. Those other races presume their races and nations to be valuable much as our forebears presumed ours were, but as we no longer do.

The West is no longer racial. It is money.

Pursuing economic growth whatever the cost because that is what we do, we want our economies bigger more than we want our lives better. If the sight of people working, cranes against the sky, or goods piled high on hypermarket shelves excites us, then we know no other senses of growth, such as family, culture, and civilisation. If news of economic growth makes us happy, then too little else about our lives does.

Only the unnatural West reduces the future to either economic growth or decay, but growth cannot be infinite. What we are doing cannot be limitless, but we have not reached the limit so hardly need care. Growth is good, very good, and necessary, we think, as if we would collapse without it.

We are wrong. Decay becomes inevitable.

Much as economic growth need not make us happy, economic decline need not make us miserable. It might, but it need not. We let it make us miserable.

Moving Money

The economies we value above all else are not real. They are philosophies. The unnatural West is an economic mirage. Economies are always mirages.

We make too much of numbers, unable to differentiate between desirable and undesirable transactions. Economic statistics cannot distinguish between constructive labour making people happy, pointless activity, and actions making people miserable. We assume economic activity is that of the markets, taking no account of most household and subsistence production (beyond imputed rents) or many of the goods and services provided by government or volunteers.

Demolishing a good house and constructing another, or replacing one good bathroom in a house with another, purely for the sake of personal taste appears as economic activity in the national accounts, but does not create wealth. If the old house or bathroom reflected heritage or the new house or bathroom is poorly built so deteriorates sooner, then it reduces wealth. Wealth lies not in momentary services soon passed but in enduring good assets.

The connection between economic data and prosperity (like that between company accounts and profitability) can be tenuous at best. All we count, by some measure, is money moving from a person, corporation, or other economic entity to another, if not in reality then at least in the accounts. When people make money from trading, any deal is better than none.

Insurance is just about money: a purchase of some peace of mind from which we should hope we do not need a financial return. If it is gambling then we are gambling against ourselves, for the most part hoping to lose. The less we need deal with insurers the better.

Gambling is also a purchase: buying a chance, maybe even a thrill, for people who need it. Money won is a bonus, but the only certain ways to profit from gambling are to be gambling businesses, to operate gambling premises, or to drink the complimentary beverages and eat the complimentary foodstuffs provided to gamblers without actually gambling.

Money moving often has no relation to well-being or progress. It often has little relation even to economic activity, when it is an accounting treatment of assets or debt. Even if we reach the limits of material wealth, we can keep moving it around. Selling our countries can appear like exports in our country accounts, akin to the little plastic toys other countries export to us.

In the unnatural West, ours is financial selection: the choices we make when our primary consideration is money. It is money for the moment and for each of us alone: monetary me. The principal purpose of money became moving it around.

Money Movers

There has become a never-ending array of people whose jobs are not just about money at some ultimate level (as most jobs are), but are manifestly about money: people with nothing to do but rearrange other people's money, collecting fees on the way. They do not necessarily create wealth. They move it around.

Money movers can do some good, adding some value to people's lives. Financiers can assist companies doing something worthwhile for someone somewhere, but much more than that is going on. Artificial hearts in fashion-label suits might not create wealth but they create jobs, at least for themselves.

Regulating the money movers does not change much. They are often smarter than regulators. They are certainly better paid.

Freedom and free enterprise are for finance service providers much as for everyone else, although no one else has the stature and scope of people with money. We need not own money if we manage it.

Bankers, investors, and treasurers are the hugest of hands guiding Western economies supposedly for everyone's benefit, but they are hardly invisible as Adam Smith described markets. They can be proudly quite visible, with the tallest of tall city buildings no longer named for statesmen and saints but for the largest of banks and financial funds. Invisible hands gave way to visible fists.

Moneyed interests dictate Western economics we have made so important, meaning they dictate Western politics. In our unnatural West, the distinction is minor. The forces guiding free market democracies are the politically and economically powerful. Whoever controls the money controls the company and the country, however they acquire their finances.

Finance service providers are less of a problem outside the West, because powerful people are less of a problem outside the West. They are not simply economies but nations, whose economies serve their peoples rather than the other way around.

Quality

Manufacturers producing something worthwhile create wealth. They make money, instead of simply moving it.

Our forebears bought to be heirlooms the products that Western countries manufactured. Rich countries retained their best quality product for their domestic markets, exporting junk elsewhere. Poor countries exported their best product to the West, trying to compete, leaving their junk at home.

Today, we malign our labourers of the past for supposedly being lazy and inefficient, but for the most part they were hard working and efficient. We paid our workers more than employers in poor countries paid their workers and happily incurred other costs for our factories to maintain clean water and air.

Our governments imposed tariffs on inferior imported goods produced for less cost. Keeping prices close to equal, Western consumers purchased according to quality.

We also imposed tariffs on imported goods, especially cars, from other Western countries, to protect our industries. Protecting our industries protected our workers and our communities. It protected us.

In return, working-class people served their factory owners at work and in the communities they shared. They went to war and died in their mutual defence.

The End of Quality

Without nationalism, Western governments began dismantling tariffs in the late twentieth century. When factory owners saw extra profit for themselves by shutting their factories at home and importing product, establishing and utilising operations in countries where labour and other costs were lower, they ended their last social contract with their compatriots and communities. They revoked their nationalism.

Imported goods remained inferior, but they became cheaper. We began purchasing by price, no matter who is selling, ushering out quality.

Products made elsewhere might claim to have been designed or engineered in the West, as was abundantly clear without that claim. That does not diminish the inferiority of being manufactured elsewhere.

Importers might claim their products are made to their specifications or exact specifications, but contract manufacturing always is. It does not mean anything.

Foreign factories do not provide the visibility of manufacturing processes local factories do. Western executives coming by for tours, meals, and shows are not quality control. They are entertainment.

The quality of foreign manufacturing might have improved over the years, without reaching the quality of Western manufacturing we once took for granted. Western manufacturing of the past lacked more modern technology, but still made products that lasted longer than modern Asian manufacturing normally does. Durability once unimaginable to the rest of the world has become unimaginable to us.

We do not care if our clothes and everything else do not last long. We do not keep them long anyway. Mechanical and electrical goods need not last long before the next round of better resolutions we cannot notice and buttons we do not use.

If factories really manufacture products with wilful obsolescence, as critics claim, then it would simply be more personal profit maximisation. The consumer's next purchase comes sooner.

Imported products might last only a short time, but that is not a problem for us. It is a boon. We can buy again sooner. Western economies have come to be predicated upon consumption in lieu of production.

Where quality was once the essence of Western economic success, activity is the essence of Asian economic success. We refuse to compete on our terms. We compete on theirs. We become like them or fall behind them.

Western economies have become Asian: cheap and voluminous. We want the right to buy and sell rubbish, over and over. Choosing goods by their price and features we will not use, we have joined the commercial mob.

Ours is a culture of luxury, not quality. A product's quality need only pass (or be perceived to pass) a particular threshold to be manufactured and sold. That threshold can be surprisingly low. Durability costs profit and revenue.

Losers

The immediate losers from the abolition of Western tariffs and consequential deindustrialisation were the white working class people becoming unemployed or earning less income because the factories at which they had worked closed. Other Western businesses came to lose because those people had less money to spend. Employees of those other businesses also lost some of their income or their jobs altogether. All the losers paid less tax. Soon enough, we all lost.

Those initial factory owners' competitors also closed their factories, cutting their costs by utilising factories in other countries too. Those competitors competed by driving down prices. Any added profit from the initial factory owners closing their factories had been short-lived.

Consumers are workers. Many are also investors. We are almost all taxpayers. We are the same people, at different moments of our economic existence.

The beneficiaries of individuals competing feverishly with each other are not those individuals. They are others.

Competition cuts prices paid by consumers while it endures, but when the last remaining manufacturers are from nations where producers co-operate, prices rebound. If consumers still gain something by paying less money for goods, they lose because those goods no longer last as long.

Economic theory understands free markets, like countries, having barriers to entry, better than the West still does. Threatening foreign countries with tariffs can encourage them to improve their labour relations and environmental performance.

Critics call tariffs a trade war, but there is already a trade war in which Western countries refuse self-defence. The Western rich think they prosper without economic borders, believing economic growth is higher and their television sets are cheaper because of it, as if that was all that mattered.

When the voices of the poor who had lost income or their jobs altogether slowly became loud enough to be heard, those same rich mocked them for not understanding how much better off they supposedly had become. People whose income and quality of life have declined are supposed to think their lives are better because they can buy cheaper television sets, even if they no longer have income to do so.

Workmanship

Tribes motivate us to work well, producing something worthwhile. Nationalism will not keep fools from being inept, but it inspires people to care about their work. They possess the result of their labour when their product passes to their compatriots: those houses and other buildings are part of the country and culture they share, as is a timber cabinet or woollen shawl.

Without consumers demanding quality, Christian faith and nationalism have proven the best motivations for tradesmen and others to provide quality work. Both are in decline in the West.

Individuals feel no ownership of their work for others, whoever those others might be. More workers than craftsmen, they simply want income.

Without tribalism, religious conviction, or reward, people have no reason to work. Even with reward, individual interests do not move us to do more than we need to be seen to be doing to receive that reward. They do not move us to care.

Westerners used to be the most skilled artisans and craftsmen imaginable. Nowadays, ours are simply better than others, but we still refuse to realise it.

People feeling nationalistic affinity with their race, feel less ownership of their work for customers of other races. To customers of other races, they too just want income, except in the rare instances their work expresses their culture they are proudly keen to display or advance, which they own whoever possesses them. Pride has no place among people about whom they do not care.

If we sense Western countries performing better work than do others, we think inferior immigrants magically become like us upon immigration. The result is local workforces competing upon price to an ignorant populace, driving white people to the same lousy standard as we rush to keep up or driving us out of business altogether.

Unskilled immigrants charge low prices to perform shoddy chores, but Western customers do not care about the quality of work, provided it is cheap. We are soon selling our homes anyway, or happily hiring more cheap incompetents.

Not just our countries become like the countries from which immigrants come. So do our economies: the goods and infrastructure produced; the services rendered, or not.

Around his home, any fool can do a mediocre job. It takes a professional to do an awful job.

A Return to Quality

Fearing white people's racism, however well-founded that racism might be, Western lawmakers normally do not require goods to identify their places of manufacture. For the most part, Western consumers do not care.

Consumed by convictions of equality, the West no longer imagines products of one country being superior or inferior to those of another country, any more than we recognise tradesmen of one race or culture being superior or inferior to those of another. Meanwhile, untainted by ideologies of equality, consumers from outside the West recognise Western manufacturing and workmanship quality that we no longer do.

Products made in the West mention where they are made, without interest whether the makers arrived there last week or however small was the last step of production there, if any production was. Products made elsewhere often do not.

Assembly is not production. It is putting pieces together.

Vendors might claim to be proud to share nationality with us, in their products' patriotic packaging printed for them at their direction, but they cannot be proud to share nationality with us if they do not manufacture in our country. To be patriotic would be employing our compatriots, confident in our quality.

Implemented carefully, reinstating tariffs need not harm exporters. Equalising prices could return consumer minds to quality.

If we want quality, we must demand it. Durables could last lifetimes, even lifetimes to come, instead of a moment, if we demand it.

The free markets in which we place so much trust, we could trust in matters of discrimination. We could compel vendors to identify goods' and their components' countries of origin, letting customers decide if they mean anything. If products from one country are worse than those from others, discerning customers will make manufacturers improve.

We do that with brands. We could do it with countries.

We could impose regulations requiring tradespeople and products for purchase to meet minimum standards of expertise and durability above the low levels that our laws now require, protecting consumers. We could end unskilled and inadequately skilled immigration altogether.

Capital and expertise once lost can be hard to retrieve. Rusted old plants without skilled technicians cannot come back to life as quickly as they fold. With every year passing since men and women learnt their crafts, the last ones to have learnt those crafts become older.

The Endless Pursuit of Happiness

Happiness was important enough for Thomas Jefferson to make the pursuit of it an *"unalienable Right"* in the American Declaration of Independence in 1776. Happiness was not the unalienable right. America's right was to pursue it.

In his largely autobiographical novel *David Copperfield*, published in 1850, Englishman Charles Dickens wrote Wilkins Micawber's famous dictum. *"Annual income twenty pounds, annual expenditure nineteen nineteen and six, result happiness. Annual income twenty pounds, annual expenditure twenty pounds nought and six, result misery."* Dickens envisaged expenditure primarily on food, clothes, and shelter.

In our post-industrial economies, the capacity to produce goods exceeds natural demand. With far more than we need to be fed, clothed, and sheltered, consumers pursuing their happiness underpin further consumption.

Without nations to motivate or console us, a Western individual's only happiness is his or hers alone. What is not production must be consumption. If we want to be happy, we buy something.

The right to pursue happiness has become the right to buy it. We have the joy of expense, assuming anything for purchase is better than anything not.

Price dictates perception. The more something costs, the better we think it must be. The more we like it.

When custom requires that we give people presents, giving money is more efficient than thinking about the recipients. The best presents are cash and its equivalent, giving those recipients freedom to choose. Anything else is best accompanied by store receipts, which allow recipients easy return and exchange. Thus the recipient knows precisely what the gift cost.

We want bits of everything, and too much of anything. We live our lives expecting innovations we have never before imagined. Constant change predicts more change coming in our seeming perfect world, in everything but us.

Ours is a new dictum. Expenditure rises to meet income, result happiness. The money we have earned is the minimum we set about spending.

We need to keep purchasing to keep feeling happy. Consumers are meant to be easily bored.

If the happiness that can be bought endured, leaving people content, there would be no call for more purchases. The happiness we buy is meant to be transitory, passing when the item is no longer new or when changing fashions or technologies make it obsolete.

Fashions are no more than self-appointed experts and other fashionistas designating styles to be unfashionable when there is no other reason to discard something. They designate other styles fashionable for which there is no other reason to buy something.

Among a finite number of choices and the demand to keep changing, fashions recur. What is fashionable must become unfashionable. What is unfashionable must become fashionable again, but by then, we have long discarded it.

Another new dictum unfolded. Expenditure rises to exceed income, result credit cards. Our credit limits are targets we hurry to reach.

We used to say the best things in life were free. In our unnatural West, the best things in life come with zero-interest financing. If we cannot charge it, we do not want it.

Expenditure does not fall as easily as it rose. We, who were perfectly happy before our latest small luxuries, cannot imagine our rich lives without them.

Expectation predicates so much of our lives, we do not complain about things of which we ought to complain. A day on which we break both our legs and rupture our spleen might be a good day, if we had expected to break both our legs, rupture our spleen, and sprain our right wrist.

We do not sit back and appreciate what we have. A day on which we earn a million pounds is a bad day, if we had expected to earn a million pounds and be bought a nice lunch.

Recalling again Wilkins Micawber's great dictum, we would go onto say: "Expected annual income nineteen pounds nineteen and six, actual annual income twenty pounds, result happiness. Expected annual income twenty pounds nought and six, actual annual income twenty pounds, result misery."

Happiness without Contentment

The most striking feature of Western individualism has not been our fall in happiness. It has been our loss of contentment.

Thomas Jefferson never suggested contentment be an unalienable right. Not even our widening plethora of inalienable rights has reached so far.

Discontentment has become a virtue: the mentality that if we are not moving forward, we are somehow falling backward. We say it of economies. We say it of people.

With contentment there would be no ambition, no striving to ascend the corporate trapeze. The unending pursuit of happiness propels us economically onward. The peace we think we have found without race, religion, and nation is not peace inside our heads.

To pay for our purchases and keep our credit cards, we need income. Buying all we want to buy can require two jobs or one very long one. Working hours become longer.

Investors impose upon companies an uncompromising commitment to profit. Managers impose it upon employees. They raise their demands, upon which their incomes and sometimes bonuses depend.

Unfettered free markets subsume us: work without end. Time away from work is euphemistically called life. Work–life balance (always placing work before life) means not letting life impinge upon work.

We no longer have careers. We have recurrence: economics

without end.

We return to our desks and other workplaces, where we put up with people we otherwise would not tolerate in order to earn money to buy things for the relief those things accord, when too little else about our unnatural lives consoles us. As such, work makes us free.

Our unnatural West is too commercial to enjoy: a place to work and fret, until we buy our next redemption. We compete for more of everything too insecure to enjoy what we have, worried about losing it.

Instead of applying our wealth and sciences to make our good lives easier, perhaps even better, we work as we do not need to work. We waste time buying possessions giving us too little pleasure. We earn unnecessary money, buying products and services we do not need to buy.

We have made money the means not just of our fun, freedom, and power, but of our subservience. We work in jobs we don't like to buy goods and services we don't want. We become trapped in our jobs needing money, unwilling to escape.

Without races and religion to save us, Western individualism imprisons us no less than Marxist communism imprisoned Eastern Europe. Only the gaolers changed.

Commercial Propaganda

Economics was supposed to be the means by which we develop and allocate finite resources among ourselves. It has become the means of importing what we do not want, while persuading each other we need it.

What remains in much of the West without manufacturing is what we call service economies, without jobs that dirty our hands. We also call them advanced economies, because they are ours. We continue carrying out research and development, but having developed technologies, we give away much of our learning and expertise for too little return.

Beyond that, the unnatural West is just marketing. It is all we do. Marketing is everything and everything marketing. Little wonder the West became superficial.

Propaganda is no less propaganda for coming from something

other than government. Our right of free speech is the right of businesses to market their products, corrupting consumers exercising our rights to decide.

We believe them, never more trusting than we are of advertisements. Prosperity, even survival, we think depends upon purchase and sale.

Relentless consumer marketing guides us to buy what maximises vendors' profits: maximum returns for minimum costs of production. Businesses convince us they provide quality.

Consumer marketing inflates consumer demand for more products, which only buying those products might quench. Consumer advertisements and our great discontent redefine what is necessary from the simple food, clothing, and shelter we really need to an abundance of goods and services we think we need.

The few items people actually need are not enough to satisfy vendors' desires to sell products. No amounts are. Without marketing, some people might not buy anything.

If advertisements did not manipulate people into wanting something they otherwise would not want, advertisers would not bother, unless the purpose of advertising really is to satisfy advertisers' egos: seeing their products in public. Simply being liked does not matter. Advertisers want sales.

Commercial advertising abounds. Governments and other advertisers usurp every street space and computer corner. If someone learns how to interrupt another person's sleep with advertisement breaks, then sellers will do so. Captions can run along the sides of our dreams.

Advertising posters in railway stations are less of a concern, because railway stations have become ugly and bland. Ideally, we would ban boring posters, to use the walls for art or architecture pleasant to see.

Advertisements are often nice fantasies. They are fantasies nevertheless.

Western consumer laws make lying illegal in commercial (although not political) advertisements. They do not prohibit advertisements promoting immorality, rudeness, selfishness, and other individualism.

Marketing, like other propaganda, begins best with the young. Like most of our actions, we do it all very well, forever pressing consumer expectations upward.

Advertisers work hard to convince us what makes us happy. Advertising allows and inspires all the happiness and other emotion lost from the rest of our lives.

All most modern marketing really promises the buyer of a product or service is happiness. In spite of the lies in a slogan, the falsehoods in a brand name, the promise becomes self-fulfilling. Compliant consumers feel the happiness for which we yearn.

We pretend, convincing each other that everything is wonderful because of the things we can buy. Ours are spin economies, dependent upon pretence to get us through our next transaction.

Freedom from Advertising

In the late eighteenth century, political economist Adam Smith seems never to have imagined the power of some people centuries later to affect other people's choices. Too self-certain to notice others moulding our choices for us, we pride ourselves on our rights to choose what we want, but we lack the opportunity to find what makes us happy, even content, aside from products for sale.

A rather nice right would be a right to escape advertisers' influence: freedom from speech, freedom from advertising. Whenever our innate human desires are free to unfold, grow, and flower without being manipulated by self-serving others, Smith would be pleased.

When professional associations prohibited their members from advertising, it did not just maintain the esteem and even aura of that profession. Nor did it only protect that profession from the public thinking those members were motivated merely by money, as advertisers normally were. It also saved all the members of that profession from the costs of advertising.

A rare product that became subject to restrictions upon advertising is tobacco, as its harmful effects became known through the twentieth century. Opposing laws restricting their rights to advertise, tobacco companies did not just cite their rights to free speech. They claimed that tobacco advertising did not increase the overall numbers of people who smoked cigarettes or increase the total numbers of cigarettes smoked. Instead, they claimed, tobacco advertising merely skewed existing demand by smokers towards advertisers' products.

If that were true, then the tobacco industry as a whole should have welcomed restrictions upon advertising. Restrictions freed them all from the costs of their advertising and from the risks that competitors' advertising posed.

If all any advertising does is reapportion demand between products without increasing total demand, then industry associations would want restrictions on advertising. If advertising were a barrier to potential new competitors entering a market, then banning advertising would be no less a barrier to new competitors for brand names already saturated into consumer minds.

If advertisements were for information only, for people already wanting to know, then advertising could be restricted to points of sale in stores. People have already come there to buy. We might learn a little about our prospective purchases without imposition or coercion.

Network search engines make computer sites accessible and avoidable, for us to find when we want. We could access computer sites dedicated to particular goods and services, without them invading our spaces.

New products need only a brief period to advertise, even if advertisers claim every variation in a feature makes something a new product. If new products really warrant the chance to tell us about them, those new products would be news. They are often presented as news already.

The electronic equivalents to advertisers bursting through the front doors of our homes are those most intrusive of advertisements splashing across television and computer screens. Television networks could restrict advertisements to the times between programmes and through an intermission every hour or half hour during films. Restrictions on advertising could hardly increase any more the product placements in films and television programmes.

The more we restrict advertisements, the more we might inspire those advertisements remaining to entertain us. We would have more to pass around the world by electronic mail. They already litter computer sites sharing short films.

Leisure

At its essence, leisure is anything apart from work, when businesspeople want our lives to be no less economic than they are at work: spending money to buy what businesspeople want us to buy. One company's employee, or a few companies' contractor, can be consumer to hundreds or thousands of businesses selling.

The only consumption of economic interest requires money. The only happiness we market is the happiness we sell.

Anything not marketed comes to lack real excitement. The sunset we enjoy is on an expensive vacation, not seized from the moment as we head home for the night. A lover's embrace means little, except in response to an expensive gift.

The best leisure is the leisure to buy: leisure for purchase. We trivialise, even despise, other endeavours.

Consumers pursue leisure with the vigour with which we pursue our careers, cramming our lives so we have no time for anything else. If we do not pack our leisure with adrenaline and experience, then it cannot be worthwhile.

Exhausted from leisure and work, our last leisure can be extraordinarily lazy. Our technology frees us from exercise, except for our fingers and thumbs upon remote control handsets.

The leisure we buy is other people's labour. In economies predicated upon rights and choices, we buy personal trainers and coaches to save us from our rights and choices.

We spend too much time and thought in work for the way that we work not to be the way that we live: alone in the crowd. We holiday to do away from our homes what we do at our homes, except that at home we live alone.

Leisure can be the solitary person's illusion of company: audiences seated around us when we are unsure of the show. It can also conceal the crowd from our sight.

Shopping

Shopping offers hordes of eager blank shoppers when we do not know what to buy, but for all its tribal imagery, shopping remains at its core a solitary function, even when shopping with others. There is little time to think and less time to talk, beyond prospective purchases.

We the consumer might like a brief smile, however contrived, but do not notice someone's name any more than we notice anything else unrelated to products to buy. We have impersonal service, unless someone's name is important. With personal services, the name is the brand, but we know little about people beyond the work that they do.

We have become unlikely to befriend storekeepers. Instead, we customise stores owned by our friends, for the discount.

Our independence makes relationships untenable. Instead of relations, we have transactions: more of our transience. Traders care only about the sales they can make. What matters are people's labour and money; markets of supply and demand depend upon it.

We collect and spend points we accumulate in store loyalty programmes without loyalty. We just want the points.

Our shops are open long hours, selling what we work harder and borrow more money to buy. Just as some people work to fill working time, some people (sometimes the same people) shop to fill shopping time.

Shopping can be fun, but it is rarely important. Small room remains for life and quality.

Some assets, such as owning our homes, make us happier. Other assets do not. We are more likely to regret borrowing small amounts of money to buy chattels than to regret borrowing much bigger amounts to buy our abodes.

Limiting shopping days and hours so they do not become onerous would afford us time to relax with our families and communities, even compel us to do so. Saturday afternoons and Sundays were happier when shops were closed and people spent time together, without spending money. Days without buying anything are days to breathe.

Power without Purchasing

Even without government regulation to restrict commercial advertising and shopping hours, consumers have powers we fail to appreciate. More empowering than purchasing is not purchasing: power without purchasing.

We have the power to step back from the sounds that we hear

and images we see. The more we find freedom to live away from commercial and other indoctrination, the more we make our choices instead of someone else's choices. Marketing only shapes our lives to the extent that we let it. Hard as declining the lure can be, we can. We can also turn away from the stick.

We can appreciate what we have, instead of pining for what we do not. We would do better to play with toys for a time and then lose them, than strive so hard to collect and retain them.

We can pause before purchase: wait a minute or two, day or two. We might then realise those purchases we previously thought we needed, we do not. Before we buy gadgetry we will not learn how to use, we can cast our minds ahead to see how soon it will bore us.

We expend time in stores and money buying gifts for friends and family because they buy gifts for us, but if we really wanted the gifts they buy us, we would have bought them. Instead, we would be better to confine our gifts to children we know will not buy them for us, and who cannot simply buy things they want.

To adults, we could give something free and much more precious than any store item. We could give them time together.

We could drink or dine with each other. If we want to spend money upon them, we could pay for their drinks or meals.

When time comes for them to make gifts to us, we can again drink or dine together. This time, they can pay for our drinks or meals.

That is especially the case with romance. If a man does not know how to express love for a woman, or a woman not know how to express love for a man, without spending money, then he or she does not know how to express love.

Standing upright and exercising our will not to buy goods and services reduces our demand for more money, leaving us less dependent upon earning it. That is all most of us can do to make ourselves economically less vulnerable.

Working Less

Our accumulating technologies save us time in our labours, not just preparing our food and cleaning our clothes and homes. They also give us opportunities to reduce our requirements to work, which we have so far been averse to accept. We can spend less time in our jobs and travelling to be there, but there is little reason to free people from work, when consumer marketing convinces us to go shopping. People paid more money to do unattractive jobs do not retire any sooner.

Instead, work could be the time to perform useful tasks, producing goods and services people actually want. Without the pretence that unnecessary working (or shopping) is fulfilling, the ultimate in economic efficiency would be us organising our jobs out of existence, with no loss to anyone.

Without protection from poverty, who can fault poor employees from wanting consumers to keep buying what they then promptly discard, just so those employees hang onto their jobs? We keep harming each other.

The continuous improvement we pursue in the work we do and whatever we buy, we could pursue in us. Away from employer demands and marketer messages, we could find pleasure and purpose beyond work and consumption. No longer pursuing quantities of cash, we could pursue qualities of life: companionship and contentment. We might see success more in loving and being loved than in job performance reviews.

Nobody needs care if demand for goods and services falls in a year, if our economic indices contract, if we are content to buy less than we bought in the past. When economic contraction reflects improved quality or technologies or when it reflects people realising there are more satisfying ways of living than commercial activity, that contraction is good.

When our work stops improving our lives or the lives of our people, we can stop. We can work fewer hours or days each week, if laws or commercial practice allow it. We can retire sooner in life, with money we have saved. We can go home.

Tax Nationalism

Amidst the immorality and folly of communist ideology, one statement of principle had merit in morality and economy. Communists objected to speculative ownership of capital. They objected to profits not from creating or improving assets but from simply owning without using or developing them, which increases asset values prejudicing people who would use or develop them. If there must be taxation, then taxing unutilised assets is less imposing upon people than taxing production.

Never is economic nationalism more obviously in our individual interests than in respect of taxation. Taxes fund taxpayers through the times of our lives we are unable to work for being young, sick, or old. They depend upon nationalistic morality for people not to feign being sick.

Taxes of one form or another are the most efficient means to fund public goods, but we individually minded Westerners are no longer a public. We have no communities and so no community assets. Even if we entertain the chance there are public services, such as police and other emergency workers, we prefer other individuals pay for them.

Ours is a selective economic nationalism. Mineral royalties claim rights to national natural resources, expressing the nationalism that wants a share of national wealth. The nationalism we reject is that which would give our compatriots a share of our personal wealth. Western governments fund more than enough nonsense to irk even the most noble of taxpayers.

Taxes can be a policy instrument. Should there be more citizens than jobs we require, thresholds before paying income tax and marginal tax rates can encourage compatriots equally able to perform a job to divide up the work and income between them. The people so foolish as to work unnecessarily long hours can subsidise their compatriots, but no others, sensible enough to stop.

In our deregulated Western economies, taxes are among our last commercial regulations. They are the purest of personal impositions, the crudest of obligations, and among the laws most effectively enforced, at least against us. Western governments impose taxation strictly, as they do not control business practices or immigration.

We are not peoples. We are taxpayers. America asserts her nationhood over rich citizens wanting to renounce their citizenship more than she asserts her nationhood against greedy people wanting to come.

Tax Individualism

Taxes have become means of us funding payments to people within our borders and without whatever their age or health, who feel no moral obligations to us and with whom we have no nationalistic sense of mutual obligation. The diligent subsidise the idle. The smart subsidise the stupid.

If governments are not going to help us, they can at least keep out of our way. The best for which we hope is that they not extract so much money from us in taxes. We want them to extract taxes from others.

Tax is a game, in which we might spend a small fortune to save that same fortune in the taxes we pay. With taxation-savvy advisers, we think we do not need to research their recommendations. We do as we are told.

There is no greater lure to many intelligent, well-educated people than saying a potential investment is tax deductible. With even small amounts of our money after tax, we are reluctant to invest in the most secure and attractive of businesses, but with the assurance that investments are tax deductible (saving us only a portion in taxation of the amount we invest), we rush into the flakiest of schemes.

We do anything rather than pay tax. In our great quest to minimise taxation, we and our businesses change our citizenship and residency in pursuit of a percentage or more. Nationality in the unnatural West is negotiable. We want the best deal.

By minimising the tax we pay, at whatever the cost, we assert our individual rights and identities. We defend our freedom against tyrants who would dare restrain, control, or govern us.

We cannot take our material wealth with us when we die, but we can at least stop a government getting it. If there were taxation authorities in heaven (and we are pretty sure there are not), we would prefer hell, except that hell is surely where taxation officers are headed. Heaven is only heaven without them. Avoiding the payment of death duties, wherever they still apply, might be the only reason some people keep living.

Not just our instincts but also our professional responsibilities to the companies employing us are to minimise the taxes they pay. Anything else would be unethical.

The taxes employees pay are unlikely to vary because of the

taxes the corporations employing us pay, no matter how big the corporations. If all we individuals banded together then we could all let our companies pay more taxes, reduce our workloads minimising those taxes, and enjoy a little fall in our personal tax rates, even if our companies then have less money to pay us. If companies want to overcome our individual incentives to maximise the tax they pay, they should pay monetary bonuses and other income rewarding us for the taxation payments they save. Some do.

The very essence of being individuals is that we do not band together. That would be nationalism.

Debt and Destruction

Communities, nations, and races build economies. Families and individuals build businesses.

Traditionally, business moguls felt passion for their business product and industry. Their passion drew investors and customers.

As the free West became increasingly unnatural, business chiefs could become like film and sport stars for the devoted admirers they came to attract. Their corporations were their kingdoms, or their private collections. Beneath the corporate princes and lords, the most sycophantic of employees became the court jesters.

With countries, monarchial legitimacy depended upon the presumption that monarchs acted in their subjects' best interests: nationalism. Corporations were much the same. Employees having their jobs because of a corporate king or queen's success provided that legitimacy: corporatism. Little else mattered.

Most corporations never became empires. Some did, which entrepreneurial emperors viewed proudly as we once proudly viewed European empires.

Instead of trying to maximise profit, as economic theory presumed, entrepreneurs often pursued revenue, possibly presuming profitability would come. Western economies became much the same.

Distracted by data from reality, businesses came not to need to be profitable, if they were structured so they seemed to be profitable. With individual interests always paramount in the unnatural West, directors developed all sorts of personal objectives behind company reporting. Informing investors could be relatively unimportant.

Again, Western economies became much the same. Government budgets became more about winning elections than managing finances or economies.

Economic theory works better than commercial practice. Mounting debt eventually destroys companies however massive they are, their assets taken up by their lenders, even if some corporate leaders slip through. Debt eventually destroys countries too, control passing to the lenders, even if some national leaders slip through. Merchant banks become managing banks, when the entrepreneurs are no longer in charge.

Monetary Sums

Finance directors do not look upon corporations as entrepreneurs do. They see the monetary implications; that is their role. The people in charge around Western corporations have become people whose jobs are just about money.

In much the same way, Western countries have come to be run by chancellors and other treasurers. Races and cultures, let alone civilisation, do not come into it.

No longer is money a means towards a business or national end. Increasingly, business and nations are the means and money the end. Whatever else Western corporations and countries became, they became monetary sums.

When all that matters is money, we would be fools to think companies are anything more. Companies merge and divide, group and regroup, form and dissolve: variations on a theme. We sell anything for personal profit, including our businesses.

Companies do not need to endure. If a company was a person, then selling or shutting it would be suicide. If the objective in selling or closing a company is to put directors out of their misery, then selling or closing a company would be corporate euthanasia, however much others might suffer.

Western businesses are often delivered by directors and owners to others not in surrender but simply a sale. There is no hostile conquest but a gleeful bequest from other people's lives, oblivious to employees and other people affected. That is individualism.

Rationalising other people's job losses when businesses close or contract, business analysts speak of industry rationalisation and efficiency. They might speak of corporate synergy: a nebulous, scholarly sounding concept to mean business units somehow fitting together. What analysts call a portfolio of businesses is an equally technical-sounding concept to describe business units that do not fit together.

Nothing is more certain to stoke fear in employees than being threatened with the efficiencies and synergy for which investors and analysts enthuse. Those investors and analysts are less enthusiastic when it happens to them.

With enough rationalisation, synergy, and efficiency, we will all be unemployed. If Western corporations mean very much, then sooner or later they do not. Western countries have become the same.

Wealth without Work

We work to earn the money we can, but if we can earn money without working, we do. Wealth is a means of becoming wealthier still: earning money not from our work, but from other people's work. We call it investing.

We deposit money into a financial system to receive more money, when doing so is no more convenient than keeping it under the bed. We are not thinking about what happens with the money we deposit.

Conversely, we might borrow some small part of the money other people deposited. Borrowers want money, from whatever the source and whatever the means, without thinking about how depositors into the financial system obtained it. All borrowers expect from lenders is that they provide it.

Banks are about money. There is little pretence they are about anything else. Other businesses pretend.

To some extent, we might evaluate our investment choices. Ethics clad, we might speak of investing in socially responsible banks or corporations because that option is there, provided our investment returns do not suffer.

Free markets presume all sorts of things about investors: we are well informed, intelligent, and thoughtful. Perhaps we are when we need to be, but we rarely need to be.

There are intangible reasons to invest money in something nice to view, such as paintings, although they rarely produce tangible profit. They are really just acquisitions. There is no point in selling anything without something better to do with the money.

If our unnatural minds moved beyond thinking of money for money's sake, we would realise that the most sensible reason to invest is not to invest again or spend more money, but to work less and fund ourselves when we do. That might mean we work fewer hours and days than we otherwise would have worked. It might mean we retire from work altogether and sooner than we otherwise would.

Investment objectives can be short term or long term, although long term is normally not very long in our individualist West. For the rest of the world, whole lifetimes are but instants in time. For us individuals, long term can reach to the end of the day. Very long term can reach to the end of the week.

Really, we only talk about anything being long term to justify the blunders we made in the short term. There are few business debacles we cannot dismiss by saying that, seasonally adjusted, they are not debacles at all.

Long term is however long an investment needs before becoming profitable, although the duration of the universe will not be long enough for some projects to become profitable. The only wealth our nations earn from other people's work is when other people's work is worthwhile.

Shareholdings

For investors, companies are not about goods and services, which money is meant to facilitate. Companies are about money. They are about share prices, dividend income, dividend reinvestment plans, and bonus shares. More recently, they have also become about financial derivatives like debentures and non-cumulative redeemable preference shares: money at the far end of a rope.

Shares are corporations in abstract. For investors, corporations become colours and logos. They become words, often words without meaning. Corporations can also be pictures.

The people who own shares supposedly exert great power on a company, determining its fate as much for the trades we might make as for the trades we do make. We are citizens in public company democracies, giving us the rights to vote with a purchase of shares and the right to depart with a sale.

Our primary interface with company directors and executives is at shareholder meetings, which few of us could be bothered attending. Corporate democracy means shareholders elect directors who report to them, although few shareholders bother.

When everything goes awry, shareholders can vote out directors. Directors can fire chief executives. More likely, the jobs held to account are other people's jobs.

Assets become commercial democracy: proportional representation where the proportions are monetary. Shareholders enjoy equal votes on the floor of a meeting but, when events become testy, polls accord people votes by the size of their shareholdings.

More like the rotten boroughs of old than the universal suffrage for which our forebears cried out from the streets, large stockholders are the property holders. Directors fearing their ouster need not appeal to thousands of strangers but to the handful of investors or fund managers they know: controlling large numbers of shares on other people's behalf. Rich investors prevail, guiding the democracy, unless small investors act collectively.

Small investors do not act collectively. That would be nationalism.

Small investors do not mind because investors do not want democracy. We want money. Investors know little of life within companies in which they invest and care even less, unless their financial returns are affected.

That said, shareholders tolerate falling share prices or missing their dividends much better if they know employees suffer too, even if that suffering does not ameliorate the shareholders' suffering. Even more than investors like employees missing out on salary increases, they like employees being fired.

In theory, Western companies exist for the shareholders' benefit, although no manager places an investor's interest above his own. No one places anyone else's interests ahead of her own, in the individualist West. He might just put them ahead of a third person's interests.

Companies are not managed for the shareholders' benefit, but for the managers' benefit. The civil service is much the same.

Without thought of anything grandiose and without the knowledge of investors, corporations can be co-operatives for the benefits of employees and executives alike. More important to managers than securing money for their companies and investors is securing money for themselves.

Managers like activity, especially from others. Investors are like managers, but without work to do. The activity they all want is somebody else's.

Employers and employees often see something special, even unique, to their industries, in which they have excelled. They are wrong.

Investors shape corporations. The last variations between Western organisational cultures are the last variations between Westerners. Some of us embrace risk, others avoid risk, and some think we avoid risk while barrelling headlong into it.

War without Warriors

The unnatural West rejected racism and collective religion because we did not want to fight other races or religions. Without racism, we fight our own race, in and out of court.

Races and religions have racial and religious conflict. Individuals have individual conflict. When we became individuals, conflicts became personal.

The end of Western nationalism and other feelings of connectedness accentuated the conflict between white people. Our relentless self-interest and disregard for others drives our dealings with our neighbours, passing strangers, and anyone else where no threat of retribution restricts us. Our separation from each other creates conflicts unprecedented in history.

Work became warfare. Reason may be part of the battle, a fervent tussle of the minds. If reason should fail, then people bully and bluff. Emotion becomes part of the stakes: the thrill of a victory, the pain of defeat. Behind company lines, tiny generals play pinochle to the death.

They are battles for people without anything useful to do: no families to make, no countries to keep. They are thoughts for people without anything useful to think.

We couch everything in terms of business necessity, but

optimum outcomes are optimum to each of us acting alone, for no other reason than our desires. Economic efficiency is for theorists working with books, something we cite when it suits us.

What happens between people happens between companies. Our warfare is war without warriors, cleverly combining the wars of the writs with the wars of the wallets. Lawyers become warring intermediaries between warring clients. Advisors, lawyers, and accountants fight litigation from behind computer terminals, firing documents and correspondence.

Not everyone is a warrior. Some people are simply survivors.

The boldness of rich corporate warriors conceals the fragility people can be, even people of privilege. Rationally pursuing more money does not mean we can spend away irrational fears.

Corporate Raiders

Entrepreneurs creating businesses create wealth, if the businesses are worthwhile. Other entrepreneurs do not create wealth but collect it, if their entrepreneurship is simply collecting other people's businesses.

Big amounts of money paid for businesses create a bigger sense of what those businesses are worth. The more money paid to vendors for those businesses, then the more money raised from investors to fund the acquisition of those businesses, the more fees earned raising that money, and the more fees earned managing the businesses afterwards. They all make at the end of the day for a bigger company by market capitalisation.

Nothing about the businesses needs to have changed. No wealth needs to have been created, but just moved around.

Colloquially called corporate raiders, some acquirers make no pretence of managing the companies they control, in any conventional sense. More feared than are banks, they are not invited to come. They just come, willing to buy.

Sometimes they buy just enough shares to rattle the target company's directors. They look to then sell those shares for profit. With money, they make money, but only for themselves at other people's expense.

Sometimes they destroy. Acquirers might play with their acquisitions like domesticated cats toying with rats, before killing them. They might have decided those companies are worth more consolidated with other companies or split into pieces for sale, with the resultant shedding of staff that investors enthusiastically call efficiencies and synergy.

Corporate raiders, like everyone else, do not need to be clever. They do not need to earn money from every adventure. They need only to earn more money from their successes than they lose from their failures.

Buying, selling, merging, separating, and doing anything else with businesses often squanders wealth rather than creates it. Communist dogma considers wealth a fixed sum, which can only be redistributed between rich and poor, but the dogma is wrong.

Wealth can be destroyed more readily than it can be created. Destroying wealth does not necessarily prevent entrepreneurs, merchant bankers, lawyers, accountants, and others earning fees, while the money moves around.

The people that everyone works hardest to protect from financial loss and embarrassment are not investors but themselves. Individualist capitalism is predicated upon people pursuing wealth maximisation, but just for themselves.

Charity, Philanthropy, and Sponsorship

Charity is giving money to people in need. Philanthropy is simply giving money.

Sponsorship is like advertising but for people and companies who do not want admit their self-promotion. It sounds magnanimous.

Corporate sponsorship of sporting and other cultural events is not meant to be charitable. We rationalise giving away shareholders' money on the basis it is good corporate public relations, whether or not customers like it or care.

Like politicians, company executives enjoy feeling benign with other people's money, granting favours with monarchial aplomb. Company money never matters as much to a person as does personal money.

Ambivalence about company money can inspire all manner of generosity in people otherwise without generosity, especially if they have not suffered the crassness of being asked. Forever individuals, they cannot handle being pressed to do anything.

Better than a company giving money is encouraging employees to give theirs. Employee philanthropy can be a business dictate, an expectation to which all should conform. More than our charity, we like other people's charity.

If company directors and senior executives were really so kind, they would donate their money. Some do, when they are rich enough.

People rich enough to be righteous mete out scraps they cannot otherwise spend on themselves, although those scraps can be pretty serious scraps. Their donations add self-righteousness to their already exaggerated senses of self-worth. Faraway beneficiaries of their kind generosity remain much less important than their fine visions of themselves, back at the office, restaurant, or lounge.

Charity can be good marketing for people and companies that need it the most. Philanthropy is an expenditure option like any other. They connote power, in whose hands vest the fortunes of others.

Donors buy pride, even peace of mind, in a tax-effective way. They might be the only breaths of moral conscience some people express: the only instances they are not mercenaries who would do anything for money.

Bad reputations are hard to lose. Good reputations are easily lost.

Reputation matters to the rich. The poor have more important things to consider.

Charity does not imply morality. Philanthropy does not imply humanity. Affordable morality rarely goes very far.

Being a director (or employee) of a charitable organisation does not make a person charitable, any more than being a director of a shipping company makes someone a sailor. Among the worst paying employers to low-level employees (but not the most senior executives) are charities.

Without people in need, there can be no charities. If we let everyone be comfortable, there would be no call for largesse.

Charity and philanthropy are Western pursuits. Without us to donate, charities close. Not only are we now horrible to each other, we are kinder and more generous than ever before to everyone else.

Trade Unions

When trade unions cared about their members, they cared about their heritage. Construction unions saved old buildings from destruction.

Trade unions recognise the desirability of people acting collectively: tribally. Their shortcomings reflect the problems of sectional interests rather than nationalism, and of individuals exploiting those sectional interests.

In theory, trade unions exist for the good of the group, the members, instead of workers pursuing their individual economic interests at each other's expense. Trade unions are commercial tribalism.

In practice, collective bargaining is a mechanism by which individual employees pursue individual interests, workers' rights for better wage rates and job security, against employers' individual interests. Trade unions no more exist in reality than companies exist. Only people exist.

Trade unions also affirm our unnatural identities, since we lost our races and collective religion. They are groups to which people belong by reason only of economics: their lines of work.

In the unnatural West and where there is no compulsion, money is the primary reason to join a trade union. Solitary individuals do not join anything unless the benefit to them exceeds the cost.

The right of free association includes the right of a person to join a trade union. Rights being for the powerful, it also includes the right of trade unions to compel people to join, when those people have no other reason to do so.

There is nothing altruistic about it. Trade unionists are no less self-serving in our unnatural West than the corporations with which they deal. Trade unions are no better than other employers, exploiting and dismissing their staff as they would decry companies doing to their members.

Trade unions take little interest in government regulation of business. Their response to employer abuses of employees is to empower trade union intervention, rather than strengthening laws that do not depend upon trade unions. Their responses to safety concerns are to pursue trade union rights of access to workplaces, rather than press governments to recruit and empower inspectors.

Employees fear privatisation of government businesses because they fear increased workloads and job insecurity away from government. They might lose their days rostered off, some security of tenure, and generous pension schemes, even if their salaries rarely reach very high. Trade union leaders, on the other hand, oppose governments privatising industries because they fear the loss of their political influence that governments indulge them.

Some corporations, especially large corporations, also indulge trade union leaders. When trade unions control work practices, shop stewards become de facto managers. Trade unions become corporate ladders leaning outside company buildings, with windows on every floor open. Colluding employers and industries pass along to their customers the costs and delays that trade unions impose upon them.

Trade unions are not economic nationalism in miniature, because they separate employers and employees according to sectional self-interests. Nationalism would bring them together.

The lack of nationalism that pits employers against employees also pits trade unions against each other and against their countries. Trade unionists can be as unconcerned about each other, consumers, and the unemployed as those people are unconcerned about them. As freely as employers demonise trade unions for sharing their spoils, trade unions demonise recalcitrant workers for being scabs.

Still, trade unions must do some good. Otherwise, company chief executives would not be so keen to keep them out of industrial relations.

Mirages of Money

The power of money is unlike the powers of life and death, a thunderstorm or earth tremor, ocean tides or sands of a dune. Mere money has power because we give it power, even if some of us imagine rising above it. People with money have power because other people accord them their power, often in pursuit of more money themselves.

Money exists because we created it. Money moves around because people move it around.

Money is a means of exchange. If people cannot exchange it, or refuse to exchange it, then it is not even that.

Without the choices we make, money is intrinsically powerless. Without people willing to take it, money would not move. It would only exist as pieces of metal, paper, or polymer we hold in our hands or store in our albums, old boxes, and frames.

The views from finance company windows are moneyed mirages. During financial crises, those mirages fall apart.

We condemn anyone intruding upon our individual interests, but from the outside looking through those windows at financiers losing at least something of their ill-gotten wealth, we enjoy watching others so wretchedly individual stumble so badly. People predicating their lives upon their individual interests can hardly expect other individuals to help them when they fall. That would be nationalism.

Financiers insist that financial failings are economic failings, but they are normally nothing of the sort. Businesses creating wealth continue regardless, if we let them continue, but instead we accept the fears of financiers. In free market economies predicated upon perception and confidence rather than reality and reason, dire warnings to a populace about financial dangers become self-fulfilling.

People who look upon other people in terms of their financial implications look upon countries the same way. Other people's crises are their opportunities.

Without racism and nationalism connecting us to each other, we are not dreading the decline of Western races and countries. We would not dread the decline of all races and countries.

Other races seek opportunities from our Western decline. We look for opportunities those declines might personally give us.

If we notice our wide road to ruin, then we are confident little will change until after we have taken our private opportunities for gain. That is individualism.

With Western countries coming closer to collapse and being conquered, there will be people seeking ways to profit from the process. They might bet we will capitulate a little quicker or slower than forecast, which cities, companies, and countries break down a bit sooner (selling their futures contracts beforehand), or which will be the last industries to go. Mere individuals would sell the whole world to hell for the sake of a little more bonus come the end of the year.

We have inalienable human worth mattering more than individual rights and economic data, however much we might have forgotten it. Races and nations reflect that human worth.

The nations we need are our own. If instead of our decline, the restoration of races, nations, and other natural tribalism for the West seems radical, then we believe too readily the ideological orthodoxy laid upon us.

ABOUT THE AUTHOR

Simon Lennon has lived, worked, and travelled throughout Europe, America, Australasia, Asia, and the South Pacific, seeing how similar European peoples are to each other (wherever we live) and how different we of the West are to everyone else. He has university bachelor's degrees in science and law and university master's degrees in commerce and business. He is married with six children.

His collection *The West* comprises the following fifteen non-fiction books.

The Unnatural West
The Tribeless West
The Homeless West
The Vanishing West

Individualism
Western Individualism
The End of Natural Selection
The Need for Nations

Identity
People's Identity
Of Whom We're Born
Biological Us

Nationalism
A Land to Belong
The Failure of Multiculturalism

Cultures
Reclaiming Western Cultures
Christendom Lost
Aiding Islam

He is also the author of another non-fiction book, two short story collections, and five novels.

www.ingramcontent.com/pod-product-compliance
Lightning Source LLC
Chambersburg PA